BEYOND THE
JUMBO TRON

BEYOND THE JUMBO TRON

CREATING FAN EXPERIENCES THROUGH IMMERSIVE TECHNOLOGY

JAMES GIGLIO

Advantage | Books

Published by Advantage, Charleston, South Carolina.
Member of Advantage Media.

ADVANTAGE is a registered trademark, and the Advantage colophon is a trademark of Advantage Media Group, Inc.

Printed in the United States of America.

10 9 8 7 6 5 4 3 2 1

ISBN: 978-1-64225-903-2 (Paperback)
ISBN: 978-1-64225-902-5 (eBook)

Library of Congress Control Number: 2023914865

Cover design by Gavin Renwick.
Layout design by Lance Buckley.

This publication is designed to provide accurate and authoritative information in regard to the subject matter covered. It is sold with the understanding that the publisher is not engaged in rendering legal, accounting, or other professional services. If legal advice or other expert assistance is required, the services of a competent professional person should be sought.

Advantage Media helps busy entrepreneurs, CEOs, and leaders write and publish a book to grow their business and become the authority in their field. Advantage authors comprise an exclusive community of industry professionals, idea-makers, and thought leaders. Do you have a book idea or manuscript for consideration? We would love to hear from you at **AdvantageMedia.com**.

To Heidi, my wife and muse

CONTENTS

THE MEETING THAT MADE ME QUIT MY JOB

ONE OF MY EARLIEST MEMORIES WAS OF SITTING IN class at grade school and how my mind would just wander. I would stare out the window, fantasizing about being a big-league pitcher or inventing some new gadget. I would go full days without recalling a word of what my teachers said. I was a daydreamer. I still am. Today, they would probably say I had ADD, but I just wasn't built to sit behind a square school desk all day.

One day, when I was about twelve or thirteen years old, I came up with the idea of inventing a sneaker that could make you jump higher. One of my younger brothers, Nick, was really into remote control cars. We would race them on dirt roads near our house. The cars had these amazing suspension systems made of springs. I thought, *What if I added those springs to a pair of sneakers? Maybe even I could dunk!*

I took the sole off an old pair of sneakers, added the springs, hot glued the whole thing together, and let it sit overnight. The next day, it worked! I couldn't dunk, but the contraption definitely added a real spring to my step. I called my mom at work right away to share my discovery. Both our parents worked, so my siblings and I were latchkey kids, home alone for several hours every day, which definitely helped my unadulterated tinkering. Over the phone, I told her we were going to be millionaires.

But, like most childhood fantasies, it didn't go anywhere. About ten years later, Nike introduced their Nike Shocks. I remember seeing their first TV commercial with three-hundred-pound Warren Sapp bounding down the court ... boing, boing, boing. I thought, *Those are my spring shoes!*

But you know what? Nike just did it. And I just didn't. I'm a believer that there are no mistakes in life, just lessons. Lesson number one: when you see a great idea, run with it. Or, in this case, jump on it.

Whiting, New Jersey, was an interesting place to grow up. My parents had both grown up in the Newark / Jersey City area and eventually settled near Toms River. In looking for a new home, I think they just drove, drove … and drove until they could find a house they could afford. Whiting is in the western part of Ocean County, about fifteen miles from the shore. It's New Jersey pine barren country. Apart from some cities in Florida, Whiting has one of the highest concentrations of retirees in the country. There weren't many young families, and the houses weren't part of traditional subdivisions. The houses were an acre or two apart, and all you could see in between was just pine tree after pine tree.

To combat the boredom, I played sports as my outlet, but I had just one friend, Jay, to play with. My older sister, Erin, certainly had other priorities, and my younger brother Nick was far more suited to live in a more rural setting. He loved dirt bikes, RC cars, and just tinkering with, breaking, or fixing things. He also loved to roam around the woods, like a lot of other kids in town. My youngest brother, Josh, quite literally grew up on a computer screen and spent most of his time indoors. Jay and I were too young to be on a sports team or have a coach, so we just taught each other football, baseball, and basketball from what we saw on TV.

Whiting was a unique place to be a sports fan. It sits about halfway between New York and Philadelphia, so we had access to both cities' cable networks. For example, on channel 11, you could find TV announcer Phil Rizzuto calling the New York Yankees game. Flip down to channel 9 and you had Ralph Kiner calling the New York Mets or, on channel 6, Harry Kalis calling the Philadelphia Phillies. Growing up, I was an Eagles fan, a Mets fan, a Knicks fan, and a Devils fan. However, as an adult, having lived in Philadelphia for the past seventeen years, I'm every bit a Philadelphia sports fan. But I'm not a fanatic.

Sports got me into college. I was a bit of a late bloomer. I think my parents enrolled me in kindergarten at such a young age because it was essentially free daycare. I was always the youngest in my class. But I caught up in high school and became a pretty good left-handed pitcher. I had a couple of looks from Division I and II programs, but Division III was the right place for me.

Unfortunately, by sophomore year, my arm was thrown out. This was well before the days of limited pitch counts and starts for youngsters. In Little League, I remember, it was like, "Throw, Jimmy; throw, Jimmy; throw, Jimmy!" But the upside is that I really started to enjoy school and do well. The college environment of lectures and collaboration was much more to my style rather than sitting behind a desk all day.

I was a prelaw/criminal-justice major in college with some idea of possibly going to law school. After graduation, I landed a job as a paralegal with a blue-chip law firm in Manhattan. It was great being in New York City and working in such an intense corporate environment, but I was already starting to realize that the law was not for me. I would listen to the older associates complain about their jobs and about how they only did this because it's what their parents wanted them to do or because they had $300K in law school debt.

And then 9/11 happened. Our offices were at One Liberty Plaza, right across from the World Trade Center. I was on a subway heading to work when the line was halted, and we all had to exit. We assumed it was just a mechanical failure. Only when I got out and started walking downtown did I realize what was happening. It was jarring. When you experience such a tragedy, it puts a lot of things into perspective and makes you realize how fragile life can be. It galvanized my understanding that we just have one life to live on this planet and how important it is to maximize it.

4

With my newfound perspective, I decided to leave New York and head to LA with only a little money and even less of a plan. I did a lot of things. I tried to open a restaurant with a distant relative and his buddy. But I found myself in a one-industry town, with little interest in the movie business. In the end, I was applying for jobs as a bartender or waiter and getting turned down because I wasn't a struggling actor. I failed—miserably. But I learned a lot of lessons before heading back to New York.

I began working in finance and held a few positions that allowed me to hone my sales and managerial skills, which led me to Wall Street, trading mortgage-backed securities. This was during the housing boom of the early 2000s. The money was decent. But still, I felt like it just didn't tap into my creative side. Around 2006, just as cracks in the housing market were starting to show, I got a call from a trader from Goldman Sachs asking me what I thought of the housing industry. *Why is Goldman asking me about housing? Aren't they the experts?* I thought. It was then that another realization hit me: *I need to get off the beach before the tsunami hits.* So I got out just before the bubble burst and the 2008 global financial crisis began.

I started working with a small advertising agency in SoHo and finally felt in my element. The world of marketing and brands fascinated me, and I was good at it. In my new role, I started to notice a few things. One, the iPhone had just come out, and everyone was going app crazy. Two, you started to see more digital display boards, *street furniture* in industry parlance, on the streets of Manhattan. And three, pop-up or guerrilla marketing was emerging. Commonly known as *station domination*, Verizon or some other national brand, like Red Bull, would take over Grand Central Station for a two-day marketing stunt, where reps in branded T-shirts handed out flyers or tchotchkes.

I started to wonder—daydream, really—about bringing together these new marketing trends. Apps were immersive, but the user was totally self-absorbed with little interaction with other people or with the brands or advertisers who might want to reach them. Pop-up marketing made a big splash, but it could be invasive or even annoying to busy commuters. And digital displays were just electronic bill-boards. There was no interaction with the consumer.

What if the immersive technology on our iPhone could be brought to the streetscape? What if those digital displays could become interactive? And what if brands could attract consumers to them rather them just hawking them promotions and free stuff?

Then I wondered, *Where are consumers most likely to engage with immersive technology? Where are they passionate and excited and have time on their hands?* Hustling through a busy train station or airport? Probably not. Shopping at the mall? Maybe, but who was staking their future on the mall? What about sport venues, at the ballpark, at the stadium, or at the arena?

I had my answer.

I wanted to take these high-level concepts and turn them into something tangible. A couple of ideas came to mind. One concept was inspired by Xbox and PlayStation, which were just hitting their stride. What if the user could be the remote control, and when they move, the figure on the screen moves. The other idea was what we came to call the *Morphing Station*. Using immersive technology, like facial detection software, we could "morph" someone into something different on the screen. Keep in mind, this was well before virtual reality became an actual reality and was when immersive technology was still in its infancy. I really had no idea how I would build any of this.

I took the idea to my current advertising firm and offered to run it as a separate division if they would just provide financial support. But it was not up their alley. And again, it was very new. I happened to be going to Tampa for a sales trip, so I decided that I would try to hit up every pro team in town and pitch them on my new concepts. It was a crazy idea, but I found a YouTube video of a young marketing exec for the Tampa Bay Rays, Brian Killingsworth, doing a promotion at a local bar. He looked about my age, and I thought he might be interested. I called up Brian and got lucky. He said, "Your timing is good. It's the offseason, and I'm taking meetings this week. Come on in."

I made it over to the Rays HQ in late February 2012. I didn't even have a PowerPoint deck or business cards. As we got to talking, he explained to me their marketing challenges. The Rays stadium was in St. Petersburg, not Tampa. They were struggling to get fans over the bridge from Monday to Wednesday. They were already thinking about ways to, as he described, "Disney-fy" the fan experience.

More good timing, I thought.

I took him through my ideas. One was a simulator of a home run derby, a full, life-size digital display where the user swings the bat and watches the player on the screen hit for the fences. The second was the Morphing Station—in this case, the ability to add virtual face paint to a user's image and then send the image to themselves via email. He loved both ideas. He asked, "How much will it cost and how long will it take?"

I said, "I don't know, but give me three months to come back and show you something."

He said, "Sounds great."

I was doing cartwheels in the parking lot. I had an idea and seemingly a client willing to give it a try. I was so naive. But I wasn't going to let Nike or some other big company take my idea. I was going to jump all over this one. I literally quit my job the next week, and MVP Interactive was born.

I wrote *Beyond the Jumbotron* with two purposes in mind. One is to share my entrepreneurial experience of building a start-up. And the second is to share what I have learned over the last decade about how leading brands and sports teams are using immersive technology in new ways to engage with their customers. I don't claim to be some superstar founder like Jeff Bezos or Mark Zuckerberg or, for that matter, some marketing guru. But I've learned a lot of lessons in building a start-up, and I was fortunate to be very early in the immersive technology space and to have the opportunity to work with some of the brightest minds in brand sponsorship and sports marketing. I'm sharing what I've learned from them.

We will talk a lot about sports, but immersive technology goes well beyond sports, to any place where brands want to connect with users and where events or venues want to attract visitors and create compelling experiences for them. This book is for anyone interested in marketing, brand management, sports/event marketing, or working for a start-up.

The timing for new, immersive technology could not be better. Even before Covid, many studies pointed out that millennials and Gen Z were looking for experiences rather than simply products or services. Post-Covid, events and "experiences" are back and back big. We all went remote, fully digital, and realized it was all way too much screen time. But we are also not going back to the way it was either. In *Beyond the Jumbotron* lies a new hybrid world, one where technology and human interaction combine.

Get ready for a wild ride. If you're like me, you're not much for standing on the sidelines. So lace up those spring sneakers, pull on that jersey, and let's get in the game.

CHAPTER 1

JUST DOING IT

lot of the Tampa Bay Rays HQ, reality set in. And not the virtual kind. How was I going to build this, and how was I going to pay for it all?

BUILDING OUR FIRST MORPHING STATION

My rough-and-tumble brother, Nick, referred me to a friend of his who was willing to loan me money for my new venture. This friend lent me just enough money for hardware. I also found a partner to help build the Morphing Station, but we were really starting from scratch. This type of technology just didn't exist off the shelf back then. The Morphing Station was designed as a seven-foot-tall multi-touch kiosk, where a user could add virtual face paint to their image and then send the photo to their email address, where they could download the photo and share it on social media. It was like a face-filter photo booth.

I found a fabricator in Chicago who was just starting to build kiosks. But they could just provide the cabinet and, helpfully, a design template. I still needed to find another company to provide the digital display, so I found a wholesaler that resold Samsung displays. The screens needed to be touch enabled, and those were not readily available either. An infrared bezel had to be added to the top layer of the screen, so I found a provider of those.

I was literally in my studio in Philadelphia building all this by hand, hot gluing the bezel to the screen, assembling the cabinet, building our own computer, and then figuring out what cameras to use: webcams, 3D cams, etc. Like Dr. Frankenstein's creation, the Morphing Station was starting to come to life.

Meanwhile, I was running around talking to prospective investors, friends, family—anyone to raise money. I was at a conference in Boston when one investor summoned me back to New York with good news. He had a term sheet for me and promises of a $1 million investment. I caught the next shuttle back to JFK. As the investor sat down and explained to me the terms of the investment, he started by drawing a triangle on a piece of paper. I immediately interrupted him and said, "That looks like a pyramid scheme." He smirked and insisted I was being ignorant. The investment never panned out, and good thing too. That investor later spent time in federal prison for running penny stock pump-and-dump schemes.

After three months, as promised, we were ready to show our new Morphing Station to the Tampa Bay Rays. But there was only one problem. Our client, Brian Killingsworth, had left to join another team.

It was a gut punch, but there was literally nothing stopping me because, for the first time in my life, I felt that failure was not an option. Looking back, I can see I was so ignorant. It was like irrational confidence, but by that point, I was such a believer in this new technology and the opportunities it presented. I thought, *This* has *to work*.

> THERE WAS LITERALLY NOTHING STOPPING ME BECAUSE, FOR THE FIRST TIME IN MY LIFE, I FELT THAT FAILURE WAS NOT AN OPTION.

Besides, I had been spending every waking hour making phone calls and taking meetings in Manhattan to pitch my new product. I wanted to start at the league level—NBA, MLB, NFL, etc.—and most of their offices were in New York City. I knew there was opportunity there. One of the investors I spoke with didn't provide money, but he did get me a meeting with a senior marketing executive at the National Basketball Association (NBA), Mark Tatum, who is now the deputy commissioner of the league.

THE NBA JAM SESSION

At Mark's swank offices in New York City, I pitched him just what I had shown the Tampa Bay Rays, but this time with images of a real product, the Morphing Station. Prior to the meeting, I was able to work with a freelance designer, Gavin Renwick, who helped me with the presentation and who is now MVP Interactive's creative director. I explained to Mark how we could provide this amazing immersive experience for the NBA fan. More importantly, we could collect a lot of data. The user would interact with our technology but also enter their contact information and agree to share that information with the NBA, which could then be entered into their customer relationship management (CRM) system and used for remarketing purposes. On top of this, by leveraging cutting-edge facial detection software, we could provide sponsors with information about how many people physically viewed the experience. You weren't just giving away free stuff; you were creating a long-term connection with the customer. Mark said it sounded great but that he was focused on large-scale global marketing campaigns. Still, he agreed to set up a meeting with the NBA's event marketing team.

A week later, I was back in New York at the NBA offices to meet with the event marketing team. They explained to me that they had one event every year where they take over an entire city for the All-Star Game. They call it Jam Session. While the NBA regionals and finals are great for local teams and national TV audiences, from a league perspective, Jam Session is like their Super Bowl. They told me they were really interested in my ideas and asked me to come back with some tangible concepts that could be showcased at the upcoming Jam Session in Houston, which was to take place over Presidents' Day weekend in 2013.

I went back to brainstorm with my team. By this time, I had a small group of people around me, most of them working for free. Anyone running a start-up knows that, in those early days, you get either the scoundrels or the angels. The scoundrels will try to swindle you at every turn. The angels will turn up unexpectedly and help you make your vision a reality. And sometimes it's hard to tell the difference up front. Everyone arrives looking like an angel; some depart a scoundrel. But thank God for the angels.

We needed to come up with a new idea for the NBA. There's no face paint in basketball. We came up with the idea of a digital bobblehead. The user touches the screen to choose their team and uniform and add a hair style, and then the screen takes their picture and turns them into a plastic-looking bobblehead. They can then send the image to their email address.

We took it back to the NBA event marketing team, and they loved it. "This is perfect," they said. We began to set up a vendor agreement with the NBA. I thought, *OMG, our first contract.* But then they explained that they could not actually pay us. They would give us free tickets to everything, the All-Star Game, the Dunk Contest, the Jam Session—everything. And, more importantly, they would give us space on the concourse to display our bobblehead kiosk.

I said, "All right, let's do it." I just believed in it so much.

I found a sales guy—an angel, really—Billy Bellatty, who was willing to work on 100 percent commission for the first six months. He was such a believer. He's still with me today as vice president of brand partnerships. I told him, "Your mission for the next two months is to find every business in Houston, every sports team, and just use this event as your meeting place." And that is exactly what he did.

When it came down to the big event, we shipped our Morphing Station down to the convention center in Houston, but when it got there, somehow it got lost. No one could find it. Eventually, they did. I had never worked an event like this and had no idea of all the different unions, rules, and bureaucracy that was involved. But finally, we got it all set up and the NBA was gracious enough to place us right next to the NBA Legends autograph table.

> **THIS WAS OUR GO-FOR-BROKE MOMENT. LITERALLY. I WAS OUT OF MONEY.**

This was our go-for-broke moment. Literally. I was out of money. I barely had enough to get back to Philadelphia. Jam Session is like a casino for four days. It's just insane. As fans started to stream into the convention center, a few of them walked over to our bobblehead kiosk. Soon, a line formed. For most of Jam Session, there was a line twenty, thirty, or forty people deep. To them, the technology was like NASA. For me, it was like the moment of a lifetime.

Soon, thanks to Billy's efforts, the sponsors started drifting over. Sprint came over. Then Capital One. They were like, "What is this?" Then the sports teams followed, the Houston Texans and the Houston Astros. None of them had ever seen anything like it.

It wasn't just about the cool technology and the forty-deep line of fans waiting to use it. It was about the data. I flipped open my laptop and started showing the sponsors and sports teams the data we were collecting. I showed them our dashboard, which showed the number of users, the number of photos sent, and then what happened afterward. This was a new concept at the time, but we were able to show social shares, the number of times a user had posted the image to Facebook and how many had shared it afterward. Facebook was really the only game in town back then. For most of the weekend, our hashtag, #jamsessionbobble, was outperforming the NBA's hashtag, #jamsession.

Billy then found someone from the Houston Rockets, who brought over the banking partner of the NBA, BBVA Compass. They were the league-wide banking partner. They came over, saw the technology, saw the engagement of fans, saw the data we were collecting, and, basically, we walked away with a $100,000 contract. MVP Interactive was now not just an idea. It was a business.

CHAPTER 2

THE EVOLVING WORLD OF SPORTS MARKETING AND ADVERTISING

THE THREE MS OF MARKETING

I hardly consider myself an advertising or marketing guru, but when you work in any field of sports marketing or brand management, it's good to get a handle on the basics. I think of marketing and advertising in terms of the three *Ms*: *message*, *medium*, and *metrics*.

The message is the brand promise to consumers. The medium is how that message reaches consumers, whether via traditional TV advertising; via print advertising in newspapers or magazines; or via newer forms of digital advertising such as search, video, or social media. The metrics are what advertisers, properties, and brands use to reach and target their audiences and to measure the effectiveness of their advertisements.

The three *Ms* are in a state of constant and rapid evolution, and if there is one thing I have learned over the last decade, it is that trends can change quickly and technology moves even faster. What was once the "next big thing" can quickly fizzle out, and what was once old can become new again.

THE MESSAGE

The marketing message is certainly changing. Philip Kotler, a marketing professor at the Kellogg School of Management at Northwestern University, is considered the "father of modern marketing" for publishing his classic textbook, *Marketing Management*, in 1967.[1] The book is now in its sixteenth edition, and Kotler is still going strong. In a recent interview for the online magazine *Kellogg Insight*,[2] Kotler spoke about how the message of advertising has changed. "In the old

---

1   Philip Kotler et al., *Marketing Management*, Global Edition, 16th ed. (Hoboken, NJ: Pearson Education, 2021).

2   "How Has Marketing Changed over the Last Half Century?" *Kellogg Insight*, January 21, 2022.

days, a brand simply told you what the product is and does and how it's priced. But today, a brand is the company's promise to deliver a specific benefit that addresses a particular need of its customers. Moreover, the promise of many brands extends beyond functionality and reflects certain aspects of customers' identity."

As his coauthor, Alexander Chernev, further explains in the interview, "Customers are looking beyond functionality for something that is meaningful. It is also about who the company behind the product is and what the company stands for." In other words, Chernev is arguing, it's not just about the product anymore; it's about the experience it delivers, the feeling you get when using the product. We will discuss this further below in terms of how brands and sports teams are deploying "experiential" marketing to better engage with their fans and customers.

The message, though, is also staying the same. Kotler and Chernev maintain that there is one concept that has remained consistent across all sixteen editions of their classic textbook: a focus on value creation. "Big data, social media, and sophisticated e-commerce has not changed the fact that a key purpose of any company is to create value for its customers," says Kotler in an interview in *Kellogg Insight*. "Value creation is at the core of our approach to the new edition," continues his coauthor Chernev. "Marketing is all about understanding, designing, communicating and delivering value. This is the foundation of marketing strategy and has not changed with time."

THE MEDIUM

The marketing medium, of course, is also changing. According to the most recent Dentsu Global Ad Spend Report,[3] advertisers worldwide spent over $800 billion on advertising in 2021, the highest year on

---

3   "Global Ad Spend Report," Dentsu Global, July 12, 2022.

record. Digital advertising spend is now, by far, the largest category, representing more than half the total, followed by TV, print, out-of-home, and radio.

It's amazing how quickly this has all changed. According to an infographic on the evolution of advertising from 1980 to 2020 from the online magazine *Raconteur*,[4] just over twenty years ago, print advertising in newspapers and magazines still ruled the roost, only passed by TV advertising in the year 2000. From there, print started its long, steady decline. Meanwhile, TV peaked in 2008, started to decline, and was soon passed in aggregate by digital media comprising search, social media, e-commerce, and online video. More recently, social media has stagnated while online video driven by TikTok has surged. The medium continues to change.

However, the medium is also staying the same. While many industry pundits have long been touting the triumph of digital over traditional advertising, a recent study suggests that the pendulum may be swinging back the other way. An article in the *Harvard Business Review* titled "Why Marketers Are Returning to Traditional Advertising"[5] cites the latest CMO Survey that shows advertisers planning to increase their spend on traditional advertising for the first time in a decade. Consumer goods products, for example, plan to increase their spend on traditional advertising by over 10 percent in the coming year. And, ironically, companies that sell exclusively on the internet are planning an increase of more than 11 percent.

The authors of the article cite a number of reasons for this shift. One, consumers find many digital ads annoying and invasive, when either trying to read something online or trying to watch a video on

---

4   "Ad Evolution 1980–2020," infographic, *Raconteur*, 2020.

5   Christine Moorman, Megan Ryan, and Nader Tavassoli, "Why Marketers Are Returning to Traditional Advertising," *Harvard Business Review*, April 29, 2022, https://hbr.org/2022/04/why-marketers-are-returning-to-traditional-advertising.

their mobile phone. Two, ad execs have grown frustrated with unreliable measures of customer engagement such as views or clicks, knowing that they can be influenced by spambots or fake accounts. And three, privacy changes, driven by laws or company policy, are making it much more difficult to track and target consumers in the digital world.

No one believes that the digital revolution is over, but chief marketing officers are getting smarter about how they deploy digital advertising in an integrated marketing campaign. As the authors conclude, "When used together, traditional and digital marketing can

> **WHAT'S OLD CAN BECOME NEW AGAIN, AND WHAT'S REALLY NEEDED IS AN INTEGRATED, HOLISTIC APPROACH.**

reach more audiences, build and keep trust, and motivate buying from consumers who otherwise might tune out marketing messages." In other words, what's old can become new again, and what's really needed is an integrated, holistic approach, one that uses multiple media channels and tools to achieve its marketing objectives. This all comes in to play, as we discuss further in the following pages, in terms of how leading brands incorporate immersive technology into their overall advertising strategies.

THE METRICS

The metrics are also changing. We have come a long way since the old adage: "I know that half my advertising budget is wasted. I just don't know which half." Advertisers have grown increasingly sophisticated about capturing, measuring, and analyzing the effectiveness of their ads. Nielsen ratings, in the days when TV was king, gave an approximation of the size of an audience viewing an ad but hardly its impact or effectiveness. As digital advertising grew, measures like views, clicks, or impressions seemed to offer the promise of reliable measures of consumer reach, but these, too, have recently been called in to question, both for their reliability and effectiveness. Now brands are looking to measure engagement and starting to capture things like "attention metrics." Again, we will discuss more of this as it relates to creating immersive, on-site experiences for fans and consumers.

Whatever part of the marketing and advertising ecosystem you inhabit, it's critical that you understand how it all works together in the eyes of CMOs and brand managers. Leading advertisers are running integrated campaigns, combining both digital and traditional media to find, target, and effectively reach customers with the right message wherever they are and on whatever platform they are using. If you don't fully understand and appreciate where you and your firm fit into one of these integrated marketing campaigns, you may be left out of it.

THE GENESIS OF IMMERSIVE TECHNOLOGY IN THE OUT-OF-HOME ADVERTISING MARKET

The world that we inhabit at MVP Interactive is generally considered to be part of the out-of-home advertising category, although, as you shall see, we also touch on mobile and digital advertising as well. And while out-of-home is lower on the ad-spending table, it still represents over $35 billion of global ad spend and is the only "traditional" advertising medium to show consistent growth over the last decade even with the rapid growth of digital advertising.

As I discussed previously, the birth of MVP came out of innovations in the out-of-home market, with digital signage and street furniture being my inspiration to take this new technology to the world of sports venues. The company that first developed the concept of street furniture was a French concern, JCDecaux, which is today one of the largest outdoor advertising companies in the world. Jean-Claude Decaux started the company in the 1950s, focused on roadside billboards. But billboards were heavily taxed in Europe and outright banned on many rural roadways to preserve the serenity of the landscape, so Decaux turned his attention to urban advertising instead. He offered one French city free and well-maintained bus shelters, all funded by advertising, in what became the first instance of street furniture. With a focus on advertising in urban environments, with limited room for traditional billboards, JCDecaux became a pioneer in digital signage, and today most of the digital billboards you see on city streets are theirs.

The growth of digital out-of-home advertising led by companies like JCDecaux eventually evolved into what's called *alternative advertising* or *experiential advertising*. That was around the time when I first came into the field of advertising. Over the past ten to fifteen years, we have seen the emergence of many alternative forms of outdoor media. It started with something simple, like a vehicle wrap, an automobile covered with a brand. It evolved into something more digital, like a box truck with a digital billboard. At times, it could be something more creative or grass-roots-driven, like an artist using chalk to draw branded images on a city sidewalk. Other brands borrowed from JCDecaux's long-ago innovation with street furniture. For example, we no longer have pay phones, but we do have totems in urban spaces offering free Wi-Fi and mobile phone charging pioneered by LinkNYC and the out-of-home media company Intersection. The integration of street furniture and digital signage has allowed for high-impact viewing of an advertiser's message. The growth of out-of-home advertising and alternative media created a pathway for companies like ours to create these alternative engagements through technology in the world of sports venues.

Media buyers became a key driver of this out-of-home advertising innovation. These are independent media-buying agencies or subsidiaries of larger advertising firms, and they are responsible for allocating advertising dollars for leading brands. A brand like Pepsi, for example, might hire a media-buying agency and say, "Okay, we have $5 million in advertising spend allocated for December and January." The media buyer then looks at the whole budget pie and decides how to slice it up. Out-of-home advertising might make up only 5 percent of the overall ad budget, but savvy media buyers made the most of these limited funds and should get a lot of credit for thinking of innovative ways to use these scarce advertising resources. These media buyers would then seek out alternative media companies like ours to come up with new, creative ideas for alternative, experiential marketing.

BUD LIGHT CHANGES THE SCRIPT THROUGH BRAND ACTIVATION

Leading consumer advertisers were also driving this innovation through one form of out-of-home advertising known as *brand activation*. Things really started to shift right around 2014, led by Anheuser-Busch. The leading beer brand had this aha moment where they realized that they were paying pro sports teams millions of dollars a year for signage at the ballpark, arena, or stadium. And the teams just kept offering them more signs. *We can have four signs in the parking lot and then we can wrap the whole building in "Bud Light"!*

But marketing executives at Anheuser-Busch started to ask: *Is signage good enough? For the last ten years I've been giving you $5 million for signs. Great, we want to be present at the venue, but is it worth $5 million? So now*

24

what we're going to do is ask you, the sports team, to come back to us with ideas on how you can create something more valuable than simply signage.

That's when many sports teams came to us looking for new ideas to take to Anheuser-Busch and their other sponsors. This led to a change in thinking in the sponsorship departments of many sports teams. They began to realize, *We can bring more value to our sponsors by becoming an "idea shop." It doesn't cost us any money, but we can bring new technology, new experiences, and new ideas to our sponsors, almost like an in-house creative agency.*

For us, that's where our messaging started to shift as well. Before, our approach was, *Hey, Yankees, buy this.* Now it was more like, *Hey, Yankees, here's an awesome opportunity to bring the most value to one of your sponsors because we can provide X, Y, and Z, and there's no cost to you.* We would also explain the benefits to all parties involved. Most importantly, we were providing a solution to their problem. The sponsor would benefit from the customer interaction and the data captured. The fan

> WE HAD BEEN TOUTING THE BENEFITS OF IMMERSIVE TECHNOLOGY FOR TWO YEARS, BUT IT TOOK TIME FOR THE MARKET TO CATCH UP.

would benefit because of the engaging, immersive experience along with using technology that is not widely available to consumers. And the team would benefit by creating a fun experience at the venue. We had been touting the benefits of immersive technology for two years, but it took time for the market to catch up. As much as we would like to take credit for being the first mover in creating a new vertical, it was Anheuser-Busch and other leading sponsors who were the first to say, *You know what? We need to do more than just signs at the stadium.*

THE DIGITAL SOCIAL LOUNGE AT FEDEX FIELD

One of the first teams to take up the challenge from Anheuser-Busch and reach out to us was the Washington Commanders, then called the Washington Redskins. The management team was very tech focused and interested in creating digital engagement points. One of their executives had seen one of our Morphing Stations at a Philadelphia Eagles game, and he said we were the first company they thought of contacting. But initially they did not tell us who the sponsor was. They simply said, "We want something technology focused, engaging and interactive, something that has a social element and can be a destination at the stadium." That's all we had to go on. We asked for a photograph of the space they were thinking of for the experience, and then we got to work brainstorming ideas.

We came up with the idea of a digital social lounge, where we would offer an array of interactive experiences at the stadium. One was an interactive field goal–kicking game. Using a Microsoft Kinect 3D camera, a fan would kick a virtual football through virtual goal posts, displayed on our gaming wall, a huge three-foot-by-three-foot video wall showing whether they made it or not. A second experience was a social media streaming wall where fans could see their tweets and Facebook posts in real time on the screen, just by using the hashtag #httr, "Hail to the Redskins." We also featured our Morphing Stations, where fans could try on a virtual helmet, put on team colored face paint, add different decal stickers, or morph their image into a digital bobblehead. We suggested using high-top tables with Microsoft Surface tablets placed on each one, where the fans could also put on virtual face paint and create their own bobblehead.

We presented the digital social lounge concept to the management team of Washington, and they immediately loved it. They eventually brought it to their sponsor, Anheuser-Busch, and they loved it as well. The concept helped the team land a new five-year sponsorship deal with Bud Light and helped them win the "Most Innovative Team Partner" prize from Anheuser-Busch.

The digital social lounge was launched in 2014 and it became a huge success. The team kept it going for four seasons, and we expanded it every year, adding new immersive experiences such as virtual reality or an interactive fan combine. We also added a bit more "social" to the digital experience by adding a DJ to the space, along with mobile drink carts serving Bud Light. The success of the digital social lounge was demonstrated with data. For example, a company called TurnKey Analytics sends out surveys to capture the game-day experiences of fans. We were told by the team that by the end of the second season, the number one destination point on game day was the digital social lounge. One of the more interesting insights that the surveys captured is that visiting fans enjoyed the digital social lounge just as much as the home fans.

That experience for us, for the team, and for the sponsor checked all the right boxes. We took a holistic approach and created a destination point through technology to help accomplish multidepartment goals. The operations department was able to install an entirely new destination at the stadium. The marketing department got this amazing immersive experience that everyone was posting on social media. They also promoted the engagement to drive new ticket sales. The sponsorship department had the opportunity to take this concept to a leading brand sponsor and use it to help secure a new, long-term sponsorship deal. The brand saw success by driving revenues through new product sales. And the fans, of course, got to experience new, immersive experiences and to expect new ones every year. It was like a perfect storm, in this case a good one.

The benefits were also long lasting. The digital social lounge created value for the fan by enhancing their game-day experience, by giving them a destination, a place where they would want to go, regardless of whether the team was playing well or not. There was both a social and a social media aspect to the experience as well. Fans would want to bring their friends to the digital social lounge and, of course, they would want to share it on social media: how they made a virtual field goal kick or scored a key touchdown, and then won a jersey or some other promotional item. The digital social lounge also fostered a sense of community. From a marketer's perspective, as we discussed previously, the younger generations were growing increasingly averse to traditional advertising methods. For many of them, the experience was more important than the purchase of an item.

As a marketer, you need to break through any consumer resistance to traditional advertising. You can use technology as a seamless call to action, one that causes less friction with the consumer. It becomes not just a Bud Light experience, but a Washington team experience. It may be sponsored by Anheuser-Busch and branded as Bud Light, but you can weave that message in collectively with the team's brand, creating a positive experience for the fan and the consumer.

When you can engage with the fan community and lean into their passion points from a marketing perspective, you can have this Trojan horse effect. Yes, this immersive experience is being brought to you by *XYZ* brand, but you don't feel that friction often caused by traditional advertising. You almost feel a sense of community with the brand. When you can create memories based on that game-day experience, the brand and the team are getting a customer and a fan for life. As marketing experts Kotler and Chernev explained, it's all about creating value.

CHAPTER 3

THE EVOLVING WORLD OF SPORTING EVENTS

GETTING READY FOR GAME DAY

For me, the game-day experience starts when the alarm clock goes off. Maybe I'm different from most fans, or maybe I'm not, but I get this weird anxiety on game day, that I just need to get to the arena, the stadium, or the ballpark. If it's a one o'clock game, I'm going to plan to be there at 11:00 a.m. I just have to be there sooner rather than later to feel like I'm settled in. My planning starts way ahead of time. What is the commute going to be like? How bad is traffic going to be? Am I planning to tailgate beforehand or get to my seat as quickly as possible?

For a long time, teams and sporting venues viewed their role narrowly as just putting on an athletic competition. Get the field ready. Hook up the beer kegs. Start cooking the hot dogs. Open the gates and start taking tickets. There was nothing in the sports or advertising world that was touching these fans from the moment when their alarm clock went off to the time they got to their seats. Maybe the cheerleaders were on the field before a football game, or a dog was trying to catch a frisbee, or someone was trying a half-court shot during pregame at a basketball game. We always felt like the concourse was the artery of the game-day experience, but most teams were just missing it. The concourse was a dark, cold cement enclave, a place to quickly grab a beer and hot dog and get back to your seat, where the real action was. Of course, this has all started to change.

One thing you should realize when marketing technology and services to sports teams and venues is that each one of them is different and has a different mentality as it relates to the game-day experience. I was once talking to a senior executive at a Major League Baseball team and he told me, "You have to understand that for some of these billionaire owners, owning a sports team is like owning a toy train. It's just something to play with." His point was that many owners aren't managing their teams or their venues optimally. You have other owners who simply inherited the team from their ancestors and are just collecting a mounting stream of gate, TV, and licensing revenue. Or maybe they bought the team decades ago for just millions and now, through little effort of their own, the team is worth billions.

As we discussed in the previous chapter, the medium of advertising is changing with more digital and less TV. However, while the overall TV pie is shrinking, the amount of TV advertising devoted to live sporting events continues to grow. According to research from Nielsen Sports, 31 percent of TV ad revenue depends on live sporting events, even though it only accounts for 8 percent of total viewing time.[6] More and more consumers are consuming TV shows via streaming with typically no advertising. Gone are the days when everyone sat down to watch sitcoms at night. Sports is increasingly

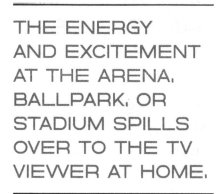

THE ENERGY AND EXCITEMENT AT THE ARENA, BALLPARK, OR STADIUM SPILLS OVER TO THE TV VIEWER AT HOME.

becoming one of the only TV programs that viewers watch live and therefore can be reached with advertising. Rupert Murdoch at Fox was one of the first to recognize this, but now every network—ABC/ESPN, CBS, NBC, etc.—has jumped on board, meaning that every TV deal for professional or college sports is bigger than ever.

---

6 [6] Ahmed Elkady, "31% of U.S. Linear TV Ad Revenues Depends on Live Sports," Videonet, July 11, 2022, https://www.v-net. tv/2022/07/11/31-of-u-s-linear-tv-ad-revenues-depend-on-live-sports/.

Despite the ever-growing mountain of TV dollars flowing to sports properties, savvy owners and team executives recognize that filling seats is still critical. Gate revenue remains an important component of overall team revenue, and so does sponsorship revenue. Plus, the energy and excitement at the arena, ballpark, or stadium spills over to the TV viewer at home. There's nothing worse for a sports fan than watching a game showing empty seats. Also, many of those TV viewers will attend one or more games in person. If the game-day experience is lousy, they are less likely to tune in at home.

TRANSFORMING THE GAME-DAY EXPERIENCE AT THE SAN FRANCISCO GIANTS

One of the first teams to create a more enhanced game-day experience was the San Francisco Giants when they built their new baseball stadium in 2000. They certainly set the bar for an enhanced fan experience by today's standards. Some of this may be due to their location. San Francisco has many transplants from other parts of the country. They just don't have the same long-standing fan base that a Boston or Philadelphia or New York has. They had to make the stadium a lifestyle destination for millennial fans who maybe didn't grow up being lifelong San Francisco Giants fans.

For this reason, the team added many new attractions at the stadium over the years, featuring great food and drink from local restaurants and brands. They also benefited from being in the heart of Silicon Valley and became pioneers in using technology to entice and keep fans. Team executives took an analytical approach to target potential fans. They used ticketing software to create a user profile when the initial sale was made, with a lot of back-end technology woven into that. Also, leading tech brands such SAP or Intel provided "entitlement spaces" at the stadium, dedicated sections for fans to enjoy. That marked a turning point when tech brands from the Bay Area had an opportunity to take a generally unsexy brand and put it on the forefront of the game-day experience. It went well beyond just digital signage to having many different engagement points with consumers.

Gone was the dreary cement concourse with dim lighting. Instead, it was more like an open-air mall with an abundance of restaurant, bar, and retail options. It was less about promotion and more about the experience. Many other stadiums have now followed their lead, adding new features like regional food-and-beverage options. The food quality is getting much better at stadiums now because they are partnering with local chefs and really leveraging a more community-based approach.

Also, teams and advertisers have followed the Giants' lead by getting more sophisticated about reaching fans before they get to the stadium. They are holistically getting to that consumer when they buy their ticket or when they wake up on game day. The industry has really evolved, now using digital platforms and social media to talk to that person when they wake up at 6:00 a.m. or on their long commute to the stadium. That long gap between pregame and game time has been bridged, largely through technology.

Teams now have full departments dedicated to game-day presentation or game-day experience, realizing that for many fans, it's not just about the game; it's about the whole experience. And technology can play a big role in creating that experience, whether it's something simple like concession technology that allows fans to order food and drinks from their seats or something more sophisticated like the type of immersive experiences that we deliver.

DEVELOPMENTS OUTSIDE THE STADIUM

Beyond what's going on inside the stadium or arena, there is increasingly a lot going on outside the venue. Cities have long recognized the potential for sports venues to revitalize urban areas, although this certainly has raised questions about who is getting displaced in the process. Despite these concerns, sports teams are adding real estate development to their growing list of responsibilities. Mixed-use lifestyle centers are emerging around sports venues, with apartments, restaurants, bars, retail shops, and concert halls. Jerry Jones and the Dallas Cowboys were pioneers of this mixed-use lifestyle center, but now the concept is expanding to cities like Washington, DC, with the development of the new Nationals Park. Ten years ago, it was just a warehouse district, but now it's a whole eating, shopping, living, and entertainment district. The Colorado Rockies are in the process of doing the same thing. Also, with the growth of sports betting, you are also seeing casinos opening up near stadiums, such as Philly's Live! or Live Baltimore. These tend to be all-day venues where fans might start the day at the casino, attend the game, and then return afterward. However, with so many more attractions and distractions at the stadium, team sponsors are left wondering: *How do we get in front of fans?* That's often where we are called in.

SEGMENTING AND TARGETING YOUR FAN BASE

Hardcore traditional sports fans might bemoan the fact that their beloved sports stadium is starting to look like a shopping mall or that their favorite tailgating spot just became an apartment building. They also may not appreciate the craft brews, the meatless hot dogs, or the mocha lattes, let alone the increased prices for even domestic beer and popcorn.

Therefore, savvy teams need to recognize that they need to attract new fans without alienating their traditional ones. Most hardcore fans are primarily focused on the performance of the team, and that continues to be the primary focus and source of investment for most sports properties. Savvy team executives have grown incredibly sophisticated about segmenting their fan base and providing value for each one, whether the corporate market, the luxury-suite crowd, the hardcore fans, the young millennials, or the families with kids. Each one has different needs and budgets, and sports properties need to always be mindful of providing value for every consumer's entertainment dollar.

For any provider of technology and services to the sports community, it's also important to recognize that not all teams are the San Francisco Giants or the Dallas Cowboys. We were once pitching to an NBA team from a midmarket city, one that was actually pretty successful on the basketball court. We presented them with what we thought was a fairly inexpensive proposal for a new, immersive experience at the arena. "Yeah," they told us, "that's our entire marketing budget for next year. We basically buy a few billboards to market to season ticket holders." That's when we realized the importance of sponsors. Many down-market teams have slim marketing budgets, but with the help of sponsors, they can do a lot more at the venue than they ever thought possible. And for some of these teams, it's not just taking creative ideas to the national advertisers but to their local advertisers as well.

The job of a team's sponsorship department is to procure and find new sponsors to drive revenue for the team, but each team has a different agenda as to how and whom they approach. Some smaller market teams will say: "You know what? We want all local mom-and-pop brands. We're going to have some national brands, of course, but you know, from our inventory, from our community outreach, we want Joe's Pizza in Columbus, Ohio." However, some organizations take a less-is-more approach, where they say, "Okay, we want nation-wide brands, maybe large regional brands, but we are only going to give ten exclusive sponsorship spots and they are going to be for five to ten years." But regardless of the organization's sponsorship approach, we're hearing more and more that they're leaning toward creating immersive, engaging, and technically driven engagements for game-day presentation or activations.

As an example, the Milwaukee Brewers were working with a regional home-improvement company as a corporate sponsor. The team was just beginning to dip their toes in the sponsorship pool, and they had a small budget. For them, they just wanted to feature a cool, fun photo booth experience because all they were showing at the time was a shower stall in the concourse. That was not really driving fan interaction. Conversely, for a large organization such as the Philadel-phia Eagles, I spent a whole summer with their corporate sponsorship team really trying to give them thought starters that they could pitch to their corporate sponsors to drive more fan experience, technology, and engagement. They knew they needed to move beyond traditional marketing methods with sign-up forms and free tchotchkes.

EVENT MARKETING WITH USAA

For some brands, it's less about the venue and more about the event. We have had the great fortune of working with a leading financial company, United Services Automobile Association (USAA), on the annual Army-Navy football game. USAA has a unique focus on selling financial and insurance products to military families. They are incred-ibly sophisticated about segmenting and targeting their customer base, marketing to members of the military throughout their lifetimes, from buying their first car or house to having children to planning for retirement.

Each year, we look to work with them to put on a huge fan experience at the Army-Navy game, outside the stadium, an activation that's all focused on the brand. We have incorporated our virtual field goal–kicking game and our Morphing Stations. More recently, we've introduced digital trivia games and mixed reality experiences, which blend both physical and digital participation with a quarterback challenge game. With express permission from the users, we are also collecting data from the participants. Users typically provide us with their name and email address and even answer basic questions: Are they customers of USAA already? Are they married? Do they have a family? We then give them an RFID bracelet, which they use to check in to each experience. It's great for kids and the whole family, and the brand benefits from the data we collect and their chance to build a relationship with a new customer or expand a relationship with an existing one. Often, USAA is getting sign-ups right there on the spot.

As we discussed in the previous chapter, online ads are losing their effectiveness, and it's getting harder to track people online because of changes to privacy laws and policies. In our case, we have a willing customer participating in a fun, free activity, and they are more than happy to provide us with their name, email address, and basic demographic information. Unlike a pop-up ad online or an ad that plays at the beginning of a video, it's totally opt-in and builds long-term loyalty for the consumer and precious data for the brand.

Other teams and brands are expanding their out-of-stadium experiences as well. When we first started, we were generally deploying immersive experiences inside the concourse because that location made the most sense. It was a safe, enclosed area that often needed upgrading anyway. Our immersive experiences became a great way to activate the concourse. But now, many teams and brands are bringing those experiences outside the stadium, to the parking lot or tailgate area, providing a whole concert feel to the game-day experience. You see that a lot now with football teams in particular, a designated sponsorship space where anywhere from five to fifteen sponsors just say, "Okay, this is my space for three hours, and it's all about fan engagement."

It is in these outdoor spaces where you start seeing different sprinkles of engagement technology and also some analog experiences as well. For example, maybe a fan is playing a game of bean bag toss with a Dunkin' Donuts–branded bag. With the addition of restaurants, bars, casinos, and hotels, this whole festival environment helps justify the expense of a fan's game-day investment.

The game will always be the most important thing, the call to action, but it's not going to be as important to the experience collectively for the fans. Some teams have resisted these trends. Mark

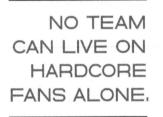

NO TEAM CAN LIVE ON HARDCORE FANS ALONE.

Cuban was famous for saying that all that he cared about was the fan's butt in the seat, watching the action on the court. He made it a thing where he wanted the fan to be 100 percent focused on the game. But even Mark Cuban has started to shift, realizing that there's more to the game than the action on the court. Again, it's about segmenting your fan base and giving each one a valuable experience. No team can live on hardcore fans alone.

SCAN THE QR CODE BELOW FOR MORE.

IMMERSIVE TECHNOLOGY ENTERS THE COLLEGE CURRICULUM

I was recently invited to be a guest lecturer at a sports marketing class at American University led by my friend and colleague, David Fyl. Trained as a lawyer, David has decades of experience in sports marketing and management and now lectures at American, Georgetown, and other universities. I was invited to speak at his class at American University, but I didn't have any real background outside of the fact that I was there to talk about what we do at MVP Interactive.

I went in there thinking I was going to be speaking to future entrepreneurs or people in a sports management class with an interest in technology. I framed my presentation similar to the capabilities deck that we present to teams and advertisers. I gave a little bit of color on our background, but during the presentation, I was impressed by the questions from the students and the level of knowledge they already had regarding in-game or game-day presentations and sponsored activations.

After about an hour of discussion, I learned their final project for the semester was to create a sponsored fan activation. As it turned out, I was giving them a cheat sheet for the assignment, because that's what we do all the time. I was impressed that these students were starting to think about how marketers view sports properties, asking themselves, *What's the goal of the sports property itself from a sponsorship standpoint? How can they view the property as inventory to sell marketing dollars? How can technology achieve a team's marketing goals from a sponsorship standpoint?* I was completely blown away by these students, most of them undergrads, some of whom had already committed to internships at pro sports teams.

For me, it was part of the motivation to write this book. Even though I was aware of our position in the industry as a technology company and as a provider in the space, I did not realize how these concepts were being incorporated into college course content and how leading sports management programs were molding their curricula for future sports professionals. And yet there was no textbook on using immersive technology in sports.

That's what excites us, being at the forefront, being a provider with domain expertise, and having that creative vision to pinpoint which technologies to deploy and how brands can drive their messaging through an array of technology or engagement points. That's what keeps the drive going. Ten years ago, it was an idea but not really a movement. But now, nearly all sports properties are 100 percent focused on creating concourse activation, on driving value for sponsors by partnering with companies like ours to create immersive experiences for fans. In the end, it's all about creating that holistic game-day experience that's valuable for everyone.

CHAPTER 4

THE EVOLVING WORLD OF IMMERSIVE TECHNOLOGY

THE IMMERSIVE TECHNOLOGY LANDSCAPE

Virtual reality, augmented reality, mixed reality, extended reality. It can all be a bit confusing, even to those who work with these technologies all the time. Technology evolves, definitions change, and different users may define things differently.

In terms of augmented reality (AR) and virtual reality (VR), many of our clients and the general public often conflate the two. This is not surprising, because these are emerging technologies and there is no ubiquitous language that we all speak. While I always try to understand what the client is looking to accomplish with the technology, it's also important to understand these different approaches.

With virtual reality, you are trying to generate or create a virtual experience that someone would not otherwise be able to access in terms of their physical location. Virtual reality allows the user to fully immerse themselves into a new digital environment, rendered in 3D or with real-life images or video. It's a complete immersion into a virtual world where there is no or little connection between the actual world and the virtual world. VR is typically delivered via a headset.

With augmented reality, you can have a 2D or 3D view of the real world around you, but it is then augmented by digital elements. This can be delivered with a headset, with smart glasses, or even with a smartphone. Our Morphing Station could be seen as an early example of AR, using a real-world image (your face) and augmenting it with digital face paint or by transforming it into a digital bobblehead.

Over the last five years in which VR and AR technologies have been emerging, there is now an intersection of the two that's called *mixed reality*. This is what you're starting to see with the Apple Reality

Pro mixed reality headset or the Microsoft HoloLens. With these devices, you put on a headset, see the real-world view in your viewfinder, and then have both a virtual environment and an augmented environment participating with you, with the ability to toggle between the two experiences. It's a nice blend of the technologies, where you can have this augmented, digital environment in your real-world environment. It's really the convergence of digital elements in a physical world.

> WHICH APPROACH TO USE IN CREATING AN IMMERSIVE EXPERIENCE JUST DEPENDS ON THE GOALS OF THE TEAM AND THE BRAND.

Which approach to use in creating an immersive experience just depends on the goals of the team and the brand, as we will discuss further.

A BRIEF HISTORY OF VIRTUAL REALITY

Virtual reality dates back to the 1980s, when some of the first patents for VR headsets were issued. These early headsets were almost like wearing a VCR on your head. The military was one of the first to experiment with this new technology, largely for training or simulation purposes. They were some of the first to develop a heads-up display view, one of the first instances of what we consider virtual reality today. The military started with applications like flight simulators or even how to pilot a submarine. It allowed them to put a trainee in a virtual environment, enabling them to learn and eventually become an expert at something without any real-world danger. The military were by far the leaders in this space. Often, the general public does not fully appreciate how much technology investment goes into the military. They can be testing and deploying technology years before commercialization. Eventually, VR technology made its way out of the military and into commercial applications, and it's been evolving ever since.

The first developer kit for the Oculus headset was called the DK1 and was introduced in 2014, the same year the start-up company was acquired by Facebook. The DK1 was the first commercial product to allow creators to build virtual experiences with software. At the time, a few early developers had the opportunity to tinker with the new device and learn the nuance of building games in virtual reality. Soon, however, AAA gaming studios were able to publish successful titles on the headset such as *Doom 3*, *Hawken*, and *Mirror's Edge*, giving gamers a 360-degree gaming experience for the first time. The DK1 never hit critical mass because it was so expensive at the time. The headsets were over $1,000, and the PC requirements were not something that the general public could afford: at least $4,000 for a gaming computer to drive the content through the headset. For this reason, it was mostly professional development shops and corporations that could invest the $5,000–$6,000 needed to deploy this new technology. Also, any necessary additional software development would only add to the cost.

It was an interesting time for us to experiment with this new emerging technology. It was not ubiquitously available to the general public, but brands and marketers caught wind of the hype of virtual reality. If fans went to a game and leading brands such as Met Life or Coca-Cola presented this amazing VR experience, they might not have any idea what it was all about, but VR was becoming a part of the news cycle and so they at least wanted to check it out. Therefore, a few pioneering brands were some of the first to introduce VR experiences to consumers.

Since then, Meta/Facebook has improved the technology and lowered the cost to where VR headsets are probably the number-two

Christmas item because you can buy them for $500. But six or seven years ago, that was not the case. It is another good example of how marketers can introduce innovative technology before it's available to the general public. Brands throughout the country started deploying these VR experiences, and innovative new start-ups were getting launched. Silicon Valley made substantial investments into manufacturers of VR equipment, such as for new 360-degree cameras or new headsets.

Unfortunately, the inability to manufacture VR equipment at a price point that would make it commercially viable and reach critical mass was too arduous, and many of those companies failed. There was a tremendous amount of consolidation in the space, just by sheer attrition of companies not being able to reach critical mass despite the growing interest in virtual reality. But marketers working with companies like ours were able to give their customers access to this new VR technology and offer unique experiences that wouldn't normally be available to them.

In the early days, we struggled to define what we were selling. *Augmented reality* was barely a term back then. We would have debates internally about how best to define our offerings or even how to explain augmented reality. Also, technologists and marketers tend to have different interpretations of things. When we started selling our Morphing Station, we would describe it as an interactive kiosk that takes photos and uses facial detection to sort of morph or transform your physical image. We didn't use the term *augmented reality*. In fact, we successfully trademarked the term *Morphing Station* to describe our new technology.

BRINGING VIRTUAL REALITY TO THE NFL

Our first VR production was with the Washington Commanders, then Redskins, in 2015 during the second season of our digital social lounge. While the football team was the key driver behind the new VR experience, it was sponsored by Bud Light. It was one of the first examples of a brand wanting to give users access to a new VR experience. But the question for us was, *What kind of VR experience?* We put our creative heads together and came up with the idea of giving a fan the experience of having a day in a life of a professional football player during game day. It would start with being on the player bus, getting off the bus, going into the locker room, and then walking out of the tunnel and into the stadium. From there the user could see all the pregame action on the field. They could then walk to the fifty-yard line for the coin toss, and then it would all finish with a military-jet flyover. It was envisioned to be a full 360-degree experience using actual footage from a pregame.

We captured all that footage on film during the opening game of the 2015 season, using a telescoping pole with a 360-degree camera on top. To give you a sense of how immature the technology was back then, there were no 360-degree cameras available on the market, so we had to stitch together six different GoPro cameras to make sure that they could hit every different viewing angle. We then used a 3D printer to manufacture an enclosure for all the GoPro cameras. We then bought a gyroscope to affix the cameras to it to provide a realistic viewing experience. We had only one take to do all this. NFL Films and the respective teams' coaching staffs were not all that happy with having us with a cameraman and a telescoping gyroscope walking all over the field. During warm-ups, coaches were yelling at us to get off the field. This was opening day, after all.

After we got all the footage back, we had to use software to bring together the six different capture points of the scene and blend them all together. One of the GoPros even captured our cameraman working the gyroscope, so we had to remove him from the video. It was a very arduous process at that time to even produce the content. We had just two weeks to complete all this so we would be ready for the next home game.

We began setting up all the equipment in our digital social lounge at the stadium. It was amazing the amount of hardware you needed back then. We had these massive PC towers to power the virtual experience. We were using the Oculus headset with their DK1 developer kit. We decided to affix the goggles to a football helmet, minus the facemask, to give the user a more lifelike experience. We had six helmets with goggles. The experience was a new feature for the Bud Light Social Lounge that we had launched the previous year. We wanted to layer in new experiences and technology each season, so this fit within our mandate. We still had the Morphing Station, the gaming wall, and the Microsoft Surface tablets on high-top tables. We added the VR experience in a new area with six stations set up with the helmets situated on a table and chairs where they could sit so that users could safely experience 360-degree immersion. We also had a huge second screen on the wall so other fans could see what the user was seeing through their headset. That was the call to action for people to get in line and try out the new VR experience. When fans put on the helmet, they were experiencing the action firsthand. They would look down and see the players' hands and arms, and they could turn and see everything that was going on around them, just like they were at the game.

SCAN THE QR CODE BELOW TO VIEW:

TECHNOLOGY IS TECHNOLOGY

Washington was one of the first NFL teams to bring this new kind of technology to the fans, so they put a lot of press behind it. We ended up getting a morning spot on one of the local TV news stations. They wanted to do the piece at their studios rather than at the stadium, so we had to set up our equipment at their studio. The night before the program was to air, we set up the equipment, and everything was working fine. The TV producer also gave me my instructions: "Stand on this X, and then we will start the segment." This was going to be a live performance.

The morning news show started at 6:00 a.m., and, while I arrived at the studio early, I had no way of checking whether the equipment was working properly. Just before our segment was about to air, they took me out of the greenroom while they were in a commercial break, and I went to stand on my X. We had maybe sixty seconds before we were back on live TV.

I suddenly noticed that the screen was not on. I asked, "Why isn't the screen on?" They responded, "We don't know; we didn't touch anything." I got on my hands and knees and started crawling over to one of our PC towers. They were screaming, "You have to get back to your spot!" It was like a prop news set, meant to look like someone's living room. I crawled behind this false wall and realized that the PC had not been turned on. So I turned it back on.

But then ... (we've all seen the Windows start screen when it gets hung up) ... the software was not booting up. I was mortified, on my hands and knees, thinking that the content was not going to load. And they were yelling to me to get back to my X spot because "We are going live in five, four, three, two ..." As I got back to my spot, the software finally loaded on the second screen. In the replay of the video clip on YouTube, you can see that I am totally bewildered at the beginning of the segment. It took me a while to catch my breath and compose myself to answer the question, but it went off without a hitch. Ultimately, the spot went off really well.

SCAN THE QR CODE BELOW TO VIEW:

Our first VR experience at the digital social lounge performed so well that season for the Washington Commanders that we were invited to the Anheuser-Busch Internal Sales Conference in Dallas that year. Anheuser-Busch's global marketing vice president, Lucas Herscovici, re-created the experience on stage during his presentation. They even took a miniature version of the digital social lounge to the trade show. For us, it was a fascinating experience.

THE NEXT ITERATION OF VR AT THE TAMPA BAY BUCCANEERS

That VR experience at our digital social lounge was one of the first commercialized experiences where we were capturing 360-degree views of a real-life environment. From there, we were able to get an opportunity with the Tampa Bay Buccaneers to fully engineer a 3D-rendered environment, in this case a part of the stadium that had yet to be built.

The Buccaneers were building new and expanded Hall of Fame suites on their club level and were setting up a sales center at their corporate office to help promote season ticket sales. They wanted to create a virtual reality environment to show what the new area was going to look like. They also wanted their star quarterback, Jameis Winston, to serve as the on-screen guide to all the new features of the stadium, which included other enhancements such as upgraded 4K jumbotrons. We went down to film Jameis on a green screen, and he nailed it in one take. They also had a spokesperson for their media network, and she gave a similar monologue on the features of the new Hall of Fame suites.

The unique challenge of this project was taking real-life content with 2D characters and putting them inside a 3D environment, one that had to be completely engineered and rendered in virtual reality. This was a first-of-its-kind experience, so there was really no developer reference material. It was a lot of trial and error under a very tight deadline.

> THE UNIQUE CHALLENGE OF THIS PROJECT WAS TAKING REAL-LIFE CONTENT WITH 2D CHARACTERS AND PUTTING THEM INSIDE A 3D ENVIRONMENT.

Our first step was to build the virtual environment of the new stadium. We took raw computer-aided design (CAD) files and blueprints from the architectural firm that had designed the new space. We also asked for specific details such as colors and textures that they had designated for the carpet and furniture. There wasn't anything that they could give us that was fully rendered, so everything was in slices, so to speak. It was like, "Okay, here are the room dimensions; here's the carpet texture; here's the seat texture." And then we had to re-create each element digitally, such as the mahogany wood for the bar, or the seating cushions, or the flat-screen TVs on the wall. Everything. There are two main gaming engines to use when building these virtual environments.

One is called Unreal, and the other is called Unity. We generally use Unity for the bulk of our development, but when there is a texture-rich environment or when you need a graphic fidelity with a higher level of realism, we prefer the Unreal Engine. In this case, we used Unreal.

The other element of this VR experience was that we wanted to give the viewer the ability to navigate the space on their own. Therefore, we paired the virtual experience with a remote control that would allow the user to perform their own walk-through of the Hall of Fame suites, panning out, looking out to the field, turning around, and even getting a close-up shot of the food on the buffet table. As a user, you were able to get a feel for being inside a stadium that did not exist yet. The team put the VR experience in their sales center and invited season ticket holders to come and try it out. We launched the experience, it caught wind, and there was a ton of press about it.

SCAN THE QR CODE BELOW TO VIEW:

We also created a lightweight version of the experience on Samsung devices that made it a more mobile experience. At the time, Samsung phones could be clicked into the Samsung VR headset. They gave five or six headsets to their sales team to take the experience on the road. And so, if a salesperson was meeting with a prospect for lunch, they could just say, "Hey, check this out." They really leveraged the technology both in their sales center and out on the road, making the most of their investment in content production. It had a clear return on investment (ROI) because they were selling luxury-suite sales as a direct result of the VR experience. Ultimately, their sponsorship team asked us if we could start putting Mercedes-Benz logos throughout the VR experience, so then they could sell the sponsorship to the leading car brand. If you go to the stadium today, it's called the Mercedes-Benz Hall of Fame Club. So they were able to leverage the technology to not only drive luxury-suite sales but new sponsorships as well.

VERSION 3.0 OF VIRTUAL REALITY— THE MINNESOTA VIKINGS VOYAGE

I would describe our work with the Washington Commanders as version 1.0 of virtual reality. It was navigating a real-world environment, one that we had created by filming a real game-day experience. For the fan, it was a unique experience because, for the first time, they could literally see everything around them, just like a player would see. Our work with the Tampa Bay Buccaneers, on the other hand, was more like version 2.0 of virtual reality. Here the user was navigating a completely rendered 3D environment, but they were not able to interact with that environment. When we got the opportunity to work with the Minnesota Vikings, however, we had our first chance to deploy what I would call version 3.0 of virtual reality, putting the user into a virtual environment and letting them interact with it.

Similar to the Washington Commanders experience, the user would put on a football helmet with VR goggles installed in place of the facemask. But rather than being just a player walking around the field, they were a player on the field, in this case a wide receiver catching a ball in the end zone. The content put them on the field, with the whole experience in 3D. As a user, you were lined up against the defensive back, and then your 3D player would run a route to the end zone, where you would then have to turn around and catch the ball. We used a 3D Microsoft Kinect camera to track the user's body movements. And so you would have to catch a touchdown pass with your actual hands! Based on the tracking of your body, it was either an incomplete or a touchdown. In that 3.0 version of virtual reality, we were able to blend 3D gesture technology with VR technology. Today, most people would call that an extended-reality experience, where you are blending real-world elements with virtual elements, meaning that your real-world motion and activity is the lifelike feature of the experience. The digital elements are what you see in the headset.

The project for the Minnesota Vikings was driven directly by the team rather than by a particular brand or sponsor. They were aware of our capabilities and some of the work that we had produced for other teams, so we were able to build a relationship with the right executive group. The timing was right because they had just built a new stadium in 2016, the inaugural season of U.S. Bank Stadium, and the experience still lives on today.

SCAN THE QR CODE BELOW TO VIEW:

In working with the Vikings, we learned a bit about public-private partnerships when it comes to sports. Not unlike some other sports teams, the city of Minneapolis owns the stadium, and the Vikings lease it from the city. That added a little bit of challenge in terms of what the team could do from both an engagement standpoint and a real estate sponsorship standpoint. In this case, the team had negotiated a dedicated space within the stadium, above the team store, that was exclusively owned by them. The space was called the Vikings Voyage, occupied about ten thousand square feet, and memorializes the history of the Minnesota Vikings. Before we arrived, the Vikings had worked with a larger architectural group that had built some other experiences into the space. One was a game that allowed fans to hit a real tackle pad and measure their impact. I think they had to shut that down because someone blew out a knee the first time it was used. But otherwise, the space was amazing, very tech focused, and had these beautifully rendered video walls. We were contracted to handle the VR experience inside the Vikings Voyage.

For our virtual touchdown experience, we used three separate bays with suspended helmets hanging from the ceiling. We also had large video screens about ten feet away from the user so other fans could see the participant trying to catch the touchdown. We also had to make sure that no one was going to try to make a diving catch or lose their balance when trying to catch the ball in a virtual environment, so we had various safety features like standing guardrails to make sure the fan could do everything safely. We have been running that experience for the last several years now and have never had any issues with fan safety.

The other element we built into the experience was using RFID bracelets for the fans. They were Minnesota Vikings–branded silicon bracelets with an RFID chip enclosed inside. As fans entered the space, they had to register and receive an RFID bracelet, providing customer data for the team. Any digital touch point that fans wanted to participate in, they just needed to scan their RFID bracelet. From a data standpoint, the team knew which fans were inside the space and what experiences they were using the most. That is partly why the VR experience has been such a popular renewal, because people still love it, even though it's now six years old.

BRINGING IT ALL TOGETHER—MVP LIVE

We capture, analyze, and present all this data in something called *MVP Live*, our comprehensive analytics tool and dashboard. When we build our immersive experiences, we can aggregate any type of content or exchange of information that the user has provided with the participation of the technology. Generally, when a fan registers to participate in an experience, we capture some basic information: name, email, and phone number. The fan also agrees to any opt-in language that the team or brand needs from a liability or privacy standpoint. That is all seamlessly integrated into the experience. This has improved a lot since I was a kid, going to the game and getting barked at to fill out some form for a new credit card and maybe getting a towel or tchotchke in return. Technology has completely eased that call to action. As a fan, I'm willing to exchange my information to participate in this really cool experience.

> AS A FAN, I'M WILLING TO EXCHANGE MY INFORMATION TO PARTICIPATE IN THIS REALLY COOL EXPERIENCE.

Users don't feel the same apprehension they might feel from a traditional sign-up table. A brand might be promoting this experience, but the user is opting in to provide information that the brand can then use to sell something or at least solicit the user beyond promotional newsletters. It's a very frictionless experience. Technology has taken the friction out of brand engagement by providing a fun, value-added user experience. Often, the first part of the immersive experience is an exchange of information. You could do it on a touch screen, for example, or through an RFID bracelet. The user only needs to register once, and then as long as they touch any other interaction, we can track the user behavior from there.

All that information is stored on a dashboard on MVP Live. Teams, brands, and marketers can log in to see how many active users there were at any given date and time, download the user information, put that into their own internal CRM system, and then use that for marketing and promotion purposes. We also track other key metrics like social media engagement. For example, if there's a photo experience, we can track whether the user downloaded the photo and if they promoted it on social media. We have seen a behavior change in terms of social media over the last decade. In the early days of Facebook and Twitter, people wanted to share everything, to "peacock" where they were and what they were doing to all their friends. Now people are a little bit more guarded and are more likely to simply download the photo to their devices. For our clients, however, the sharing is less important than the experience for the fan.

The other feature that really sets us apart with MVP Live is that we can capture what we call *anonymous analytics*. This leverages facial detection (but not recognition) software to give a bird's-eye view of how many views the interaction is getting from the assembled fans. If we have a Morphing Station or a VR experience or any other gaming experience, we put a camera to provide a bird's-eye view of the crowd, where we can track how many people had the opportunity to view the experience on the screen, capturing key metrics like attention times or dwell times. This allows us to provide data not on just active users but passive users as well. Furthermore, we also capture key demographic information like age and gender. It's always exciting to us and our clients when we present this data and it shows that female engagement is generally equal to male, which is a great breakthrough to the stereotype of sports being male dominated.

For example, we might have two hundred active users of an experience, but we can show data that over five thousand viewers were attracted to the space and were watching the action on the screen. From a media perspective, it's like knowing how many people really saw and paid attention to your billboard. Not everyone is going to be an active user. Maybe they were a little resistant, maybe they had a cool time watching it or were rooting for their friends or family members. It's okay that they didn't actively participate in the experience, but the team and the brand are still reaching them. We have the data to show what we call the *skyscraper effect*, everyone looking up at the same time. Fans tend to loiter around these experiences and are amazed at what they are seeing. And so we provide that data as well.

NAVIGATING HYPE CYCLES

The biggest challenge in the evolving world of immersive technology is really keeping pace with what we call *hype cycles*. These cycles are generally driven by marketers but are also based on developments in technology. In 2014 and 2015, for example, it was all about virtual reality. But at the time, the technology was too expensive for the general public. As VR technology has become more affordable, providers of VR technology are now struggling with a new problem: How much time do users really want to spend in a virtual environment? The idea of long dwell-time engagements in a headset environment is simply not a comfortable, natural experience for most users. I'm guilty myself. I'm a technologist. I have a headset at home. But I can't spend more than an hour in an experience, and even then, the headset will sit idle for six days. I think the real challenge for the industry and for companies like Meta is to break through normal human behavior of being comfortable with having something on your head for hours on end.

In our case, we typically create short, sixty- to ninety-second VR experiences, which is perfect for most users. You get into the experience and then you get out. Many tech companies were going to build VR gaming stations designed to play games all day or have you watch a two-hour movie in VR. They all failed. That's just human behavior. As a result, that's where AR has become a far more scalable experience than VR because the engagement point is usually just with your mobile device. Eventually that's where the hype cycle has shifted to: using AR through a mobile device.

Mobile-based AR was a more natural experience for many users. The challenge with the explosion of AR experiences, however, became what we called *apps fatigue*. Brands wanted to create an augmented reality experience, but typically it required the downloading of a dedicated app. Customers were reluctant to do so, especially if it was just for a one-day event. We are able to avoid that now by building web-based AR experiences. By using a QR code or a URL, a user can have all the features of an app without the download.

Covid, in many ways, promoted that "touchless" technology, as we were living in a world where you didn't want to touch anything. QR codes were a twenty-year-old technology, but they became the most powerful technology in 2020 because of this whole touchless life around us. What's old can become new again.

BRIDGING COMMUNITY OUTREACH AND AUGMENTED REALITY AT THE TENNESSEE TITANS

It was during Covid when we started working with the Tennessee Titans to create a web-based AR experience, using a huge mural painted on the side of a building in downtown Nashville. Users would walk down the street and see QR code stickers on the sidewalk announcing, "Hey, scan this QR code, point your phone at the mural, and then the mural will come to life on your phone." The player on the mural came to life in 3D, crushing the building and spiking a football. The augmented reality was like a hype video for the upcoming season. The team was very smart because, at that time in 2020, based on where you were regionally, some stadiums allowed fans, while other stadiums did not.

The background of the project was that the team wanted to do something that involved community outreach. Therefore, they commissioned a local artist, leased the side of a huge building in downtown Nashville, and created a memorial to the toughness of Tennessee. That AR experience went viral; everyone was posting it on Instagram or posing with selfies in front of the mural. It performed really well for the team, with a ton of press around it, and it was a perfect scalable experience because you could take the image of the mural and use it in other ways as well. For the team's holiday card, for example, they put the mural on the card with the QR code, so you could have the same experience as if you were standing in front of the building. They also printed a huge reproduction of the mural and put it at the stadium, where fans could participate in the AR experience at the game. That's where augmented reality has an advantage over virtual reality for marketers, because it's far more scalable.

SCAN THE QR CODE BELOW TO VIEW:

For us, it's always important to stay ahead of the latest hype cycle but without getting too caught up in what could become a quickly passing fad. Marketers love the new flashy thing, and everyone wants to be the first to deploy some new experience. For example, we had a great experience with the Washington Commanders and the digital social lounge and began promoting that to many other teams and brands. But then, seemingly overnight, the metaverse exploded, and every venture capital firm was investing in the space. Soon there were a million avatar creators. Then, Facebook changed its name to Meta in October 2021, reflecting this trend. But just as everyone was talking about the metaverse, we were soon entering a post-Covid world where users wanted live, physical experiences again, with a lot less screen time, not more. They wanted more social interaction with real people, not less. Therefore, we always must be careful to not pivot too much based on these trends or hype cycles because often the slow and steady approach wins the race. That's kind of been our motto.

Demand for live events is at an all-time high because we were stripped of that experience for two years. As live events and sporting games have come back, some of these older, immersive experiences are coming back into vogue because it's a tactile, physical, emotional, and memorable experience, only available when you're at an event and participating in an activity. The metaverse, for our clientele, is not something that we're too intimidated by, because we want to capture that live-event experience, and the metaverse doesn't allow for that.

THE EMERGING WORLD OF MIXED REALITY

In my opinion, mixed reality, via AR headsets, is going to accomplish what the metaverse or VR headsets could not. AR headsets are almost like eyeglasses, where you see the physical environment around you, but then digital or virtual elements can be added. Google Glass, launched ten years ago, was way ahead of its time, and I would not be surprised if they brought it back. For scalable technology to change human behavior, it must be something that we're comfortable with. Wearing a heavy headset and spending all your time in a virtual environment is probably not going to be the ideal solution. But when you can put on see-through glasses, like a pair of reading glasses, and then have an augmented reality overlay on top of that, that's going to be a game changer for society. Think about being under your sink, trying to fix a pipe and not knowing how to do it. You could be watching a tutorial through your mixed reality glasses, having both of your hands free to do exactly the task that you're trying to accomplish. Or imagine driving in your car—you could have Waze or your navigation right on your lens, without taking your eyes off the road. We see a lot of potential for this new mixed reality and AR technology because it allows you to view live events while at the same time having an enhanced digital experience.

> FOR SCALABLE TECHNOLOGY TO CHANGE HUMAN BEHAVIOR, IT MUST BE SOME-THING THAT WE'RE COM-FORTABLE WITH.

For us and our clients, the goal is always to create a more holistic campaign, where a fan or consumer can experience something first at the stadium and then, ideally, take it with them. A good example of this is when we worked with Madison Square Garden in 2021 on a project underwritten by Chase Bank, their big corporate sponsor. It was the seventy-fifth anniversary of the NBA, and so each team did their own version of the anniversary of their team. For example, the New York Knicks and the New York Rangers decided to produce a twenty-ounce commemorative cup featuring some of their best-known players, like Patrick Ewing or Clyde Frazier from the New York Knicks or Mark Messier from the New York Rangers. Each commemorative cup came with a QR code and, just like our mural in downtown Nashville, the user could point their phone's camera at the QR code and watch the player come to life on their phone, in this case a player highlight. Best of all, the fan would take the cup home and put it in their kitchen cabinet. When a neighbor comes over, they could say, "Hey, check this out." It became an experience and a keepsake that you could only get by going to the game. Once again, it was an experience that checked all the boxes, for the team, for the brand, and for the fan.

SCAN THE QR CODE BELOW TO VIEW:

Over the last three chapters, we have talked about the evolving world of sports marketing and advertising, the evolving world of sporting events, and now the evolving world of immersive technology. Each one of them will continue to develop and evolve. I hope what you have gained through it all is an appreciation for taking a holistic, integrated view of the sports marketing ecosystem. Wherever you fall in that ecosystem, what remains paramount is to maintain a focus on the fan experience and the importance of delivering value to consumers. If the last three chapters have covered the what and the why of immersive technology, we will next turn our attention to the how—how to bring these projects to fruition for the benefit of teams, brands, and, most importantly, the fans.

CHAPTER 5

SOLUTIONS AND SERVICES

AT MVP INTERACTIVE, WE FOLLOW A COLLABORATIVE approach with our clients to understand their technological goals and brand message and bring an immersive experience to life. To do that, we follow a proven process that we call the five *D*s.

This process always begins with **Discovery**. We work collaboratively with our clients to identify overall objectives and then brainstorm about creative solutions using current products or unique interactive design options.

Once we have a clear idea of a client's needs, we move on to the next step in the process: **Design**. Our creative-design team takes over to lead the UI/UX design process. The client is shepherded closely throughout the project journey, working with our team to refine the design until it meets their expectations. During this phase, it is important that we adhere to all brand guidelines to ensure a cohesive look and feel, both for the immersive experience and for the holistic marketing campaign of all the brands involved in the project.

Next, we move on to **Development**. This is where the main software development and project management activities take place.

With the knowledge we've gathered during the discovery phase, our team creates a development plan with clearly established milestones and key delivery dates. As we work through the process, the client is kept informed of progress and involved in alpha and beta software releases and hardware testing. In general, enthusiasm for the project increases as tangible progress is demonstrated and the initial concepts developed during the discovery phase start to take shape.

Once development is complete, we move on to **Deployment**. This is where the final integration is installed and activated on location. After all the logistics, operational, and final testing protocols are completed, we're ready to go live! Our goal is always to bring value to a client's brand by creating not just a spectacular experience but a memorable one as well. We do the heavy lifting to ensure that everything runs smoothly, which helps clients achieve an ROI beyond measure.

Finally, we focus on **Data**. We provide postactivation data tracking using our proprietary MVP Live Analytics platform. MVP Live provides real-time analytics tracking for audience measurement, registration, and experience-specific gameplay events. With this data, clients can measure the success of their projects and make informed decisions for the future. This comprehensive data has been one of our key competitive advantages over the years. Not only are we able to execute on a fun front-end experience, but we also provide valuable insight to the client on the performance of the activation and on user behavior, which has been a key performance indicator for ROI.

> OUR UNIQUE APPROACH AND PROCESS CERTAINLY HELPED WHEN COVID HIT IN MARCH 2020.

Our unique approach and process certainly helped when Covid hit in March 2020. As a live-event technology company, MVP Interactive was looking at a bleak environment. Therefore, we had to rely on our services and on our domain expertise to evangelize how we could help clients navigate this unprecedented pandemic.

I told my sales team that the company had enough runway to keep their jobs and their salaries but not to expect much in terms of commissions because we suddenly didn't have any buyers. Live events were certainly on hold, and no one knew when they would return. We decided that while we were unlikely to sell any products, at least in terms of live-event immersive technology, we could go offer our services to the market. Therefore, we embarked on a strategic plan to promote our services and domain expertise. This shift caused us to look inward and ask ourselves, *What exactly are those services and how can we demonstrate our domain expertise?*

We realized that when building interactive software, there are a lot of creativity and design elements that need to happen. We had unique design capabilities that allowed us to design and strategize on brand messaging. We also had unique skills in environmental design, reimagining space through creative imaging, whether it was through 3D modeling, motion graphics, or even large format printing. We therefore went to the market and asked, *How can our design services be of value to you? Are you thinking of doing any social promotion? Are you thinking about the metaverse; about how you might introduce remote, virtual campaigns; where we could help design and build a virtual environment for you and your customers?*

Another domain expertise of ours was digital signage. As activities moved outdoors, signage would become more important. We had extensive knowledge in the field along with a network of integrators who could deliver digital signage solutions. We could sell our digital signage capabilities and then build content on top of that.

The other service we could offer was consulting. We asked ourselves, *Can we find a venue, team, property, or brand that we can consult for during the next year, just to keep the lights on?* Through all these efforts, we eventually found success, not with a sports team or brand, but with a museum—and not just any museum but one of the most iconic: Graceland.

BRINGING IMMERSIVE TECHNOLOGY TO GRACELAND

Graceland is Elvis Presley's sprawling mansion and ranch in Memphis, Tennessee, which has grown into one of the most popular tourist destinations in the United States. Several years earlier, Elvis's estate sold the rights to a private equity firm to build and manage a two-hundred-thousand-square-foot facility across the street from Graceland called *Elvis Presley's Memphis.* The management team of the new attraction was using the Covid shutdown as an opportunity to rethink the visitor experience. That's where we came in.

In the first part of our process, **Discovery**, we asked the museum's management team, *What's your main pain point? What are you looking to accomplish with this new, immersive technology?* They told us that they had an aging fan base and that they needed to do something to get smart and to keep pace with the next generation of Elvis fans.

The entire Graceland complex is more than just a mansion and a museum; it's an amusement park. There's a concert venue, several restaurants, and two of Elvis's airplanes parked on the campus. Each section of the campus memorializes a different stage of Elvis's life. When we visited, we decided to do a site survey. We spent two days with them, learning everything about what Elvis was really like, what his passions were. We also asked them, *What is the goal of the facility?* They said that they wanted immersive technology to drive ticket sales and to increase engagement. We came up with the idea that we would try to mastermind an interactive experience for each stage of Elvis's life.

From there, we moved on to the next step in our process: **Design**. We rendered a full plan for all these digital experiences that we felt made the most sense, both for the property and for the legacy of Elvis.

The new facility, Elvis Presley's Memphis, was relatively new, so they did have some existing digital and technology elements, but it was fairly limited, still very analog, with just some photo booth experiences. Transitioning to developing immersive experiences was an internal project for them, and they had not brought in any outside design firms before us. They had dedicated marketing and design teams, and it was their responsibility to create an engaging experience for the visitor. The project lead we worked with was the director of Elvis Presley's Memphis, and she was one of only four individuals who are allowed upstairs in the mansion, which is considered sacred space.

One thing we learned on our visit to Graceland was that Elvis had a fascination with golf carts. He loved zipping around the campus with his daughter, Lisa Marie, on his lap. He also had a preferred brand of golf cart: Harley-Davidson. Many people don't know this, but the iconic motorcycle maker manufactured its own line of golf carts from 1963–1969 before the line was sold to AMF. We thought, *How cool would it be if visitors could sit in an old Harley-Davidson golf cart and take a (virtual) ride around Graceland, just like Elvis did?*

The first challenge was finding old Harley-Davidson golf carts. Vintage ones in good condition were hard to find and highly sought after by collectors. But we did not need them in working condition, just a few that could be refurbished so someone could sit on the golf cart while it was stationary. We resorted to practically dumpster diving at junkyards, finding old 1960s-era Harley-Davidson golf carts. We then partnered with a fabrication company, who refurbished them fantastically. Next, we added hydraulics to give the feeling of motion and of driving over the hills and bumps of the Graceland campus. Then we created a 360-degree driving experience where Elvis fans could sit on the golf cart, turn the wheel, and steer their way around a virtual Graceland.

We filmed the entire campus using 360-degree cameras. Cameras had come a long way since we had first filmed that pregame experience for the Washington Commanders. Samsung became one of the major players in the VR hardware space, and they had built a fully integrated multicamera unit called the Samsung 360 Round. We were one of the first commercial companies to purchase and beta test the unit. The 360 Round was a studio grade VR camera that not only had multiple cameras already affixed to it, but it was able to process a first-level stitching of the content. Therefore, we didn't have to spend as much time on postproduction, piecing together every single frame, as we had to do for the Commanders. That said, you could not simply complete all the filming and then have it be ready to go. But the new camera technology made postediting much easier, eliminating at least 50–60 percent of our manual efforts. That helped our workflow tremendously.

In terms of filming the Graceland campus, the camera was attached to a gooseneck, which would stabilize the image, and then affixed to the windshield of the golf cart. We drove around in a golf cart navigating the entire campus, coming up with different routes and capturing all the different movements of the golf cart because, in the experience, the fan would be able to choose their own adventure, what route they wanted to take.

The magic of the experience was that the Elvis fan was sitting in an actual golf cart but looking at a screen that showed them driving through the virtual Graceland campus. We put an accelerometer underneath the steering shaft so that, by using software, when the fan turned left, the content on the screen would change to follow that navigation. We also put in a hydraulic system in the golf cart so that the fan would feel the motion of driving. For example, when they pressed the gas pedal to go up a hill, the golf cart would bounce around. However, even though the instructions clearly told the user to hit the brake pedal before they got off, people would just get out and just leave the motor running. After a time, the hydraulic system started to burn out. Unfortunately, the human error factor meant that the hydraulic motion feature could not live on, just because it became a mechanical nightmare. We have learned over time that, yes, technology will sometimes fail, but the amount of human error that must be factored into an immersive experience is also something to consider.

One of Elvis's other passions was dancing and, of course, music. So we built an immersive experience that was an interactive dance floor. Using a touch-enabled ten-foot-by-ten-foot LED dance floor, we built a quiz game where the fan could choose their answers by stomping with their left or right foot. We even managed to factor in social distancing, which was important at the time. Four people could play at the same time, each in a different corner of the dance floor. They would each move in unison to the next answer. The last feature of the dance game was "Name this Tune." We piped in sound to play an iconic Elvis song and then asked the user, *What song are you hearing right now?* They would have to step on the right answer. The songs were "Blue Suede Shoes," "Hound Dog," or some other Elvis classic. The interactive dance floor was a big hit as well.

Continuing the theme of memorializing Elvis's life, we knew that he went from being a music star to becoming a movie star for many years. The many famous movie posters featuring Elvis were definitely a key part of his legacy. Using our Morphing Stations, we were able to create an augmented reality photo experience, where the fan could put themselves into the movie poster with Elvis. Using AR technology, we did a background subtraction without any green screen. The Microsoft Kinect camera was able to insert whatever movie poster the user chose as the backdrop, and then their image would be inserted into the movie poster with Elvis. We did the same thing with album covers. We installed about eight photo booth kiosks, and it was very popular. With the eight AR photo booth kiosks, three golf car virtual driving experiences, and the interactive dance floor, we kept many Elvis fans fully engaged.

Another iconic symbol of Elvis was his wardrobe, in particular his bedazzled jumpsuits. Therefore, we decided to create an immersive experience that allowed users to virtually try on one of four Elvis jumpsuits. This "magic mirror" of sorts leveraged our ability to re-create each jumpsuit in 3D. We then built an augmented reality application that would capture the user's skeletal form, and then magically affix the suit onto their body, creating a fun wardrobe photo experience. Personally, I'm a big fan of Elvis's tiger jumpsuit, so I had a lot of fun testing out the experience.

So far, we had successfully developed several immersive experiences: Elvis fans could drive around a virtual Graceland in a golf cart, play an Elvis-themed dancing quiz game, appear in an Elvis movie poster or album cover, and see themselves in an Elvis jumpsuit. But we knew that we needed to have an immersive experience that featured Elvis singing. We thought, *What if Elvis could sing to you in a scene from one of his movies, like* Blue Hawaii? We called the immersive experience the Serenade. We first built out a miniature studio, a green screen studio. After that, through a process known as rotoscoping, we used actual footage from the movie but then removed the actors in the scene and replaced them with a live video of the fans sitting in the studio. On a large screen, the fan could see themselves being serenaded by Elvis in the movie. Of course, the video was recorded so that the fan could enter their email address and have it sent to them for their own enjoyment or for posting on social media.

The biggest challenge with the Serenade—and even the movie and album posters—was the quality of the video and images. There was no archive of the *Blue Hawaii* movie other than what we could find on a DVD. From a production standpoint, it was a nightmare because we had to pull sub-HD files to re-create the experience. The movie, along with the movie posters and album covers, were of vintage quality and therefore had a grainy aspect to them. If we filmed or photographed the fan in HD and then inserted them into the old movie/poster, it would look rather strange. Instead, through editing and software, we were able to put a grainy texture or a filter on the live video or photo of the fan and then insert that reconfigured image into the vintage film clip, movie poster, or album cover.

The Serenade also proved to be hugely popular, with constant sign-ups and people sharing the videos or movie posters on social media, greatly boosting exposure for the museum. We recently got a call from some representatives of an international sports Hall of Fame museum who had visited Graceland and had seen our interactive experiences. They are planning a major renovation of their facility and now want to add similar immersive experiences.

As with all our projects, the last step in the process is **Data**. Every client gets access to MVP Live, where they can access real-time data on users and engagement. The Elvis Presley Experience has been a record breaker for us in terms of usage because, unlike a sports stadium, it's open seven days a week, eight hours a day. Even hour by hour, the usage is above and beyond any other sort of concourse activation that we've done for sports teams because it's not just three hours of a game-day experience. Also, every museum visitor who comes through the doors is exposed to the interactive experiences. The performance has been proved with key performance indicators (KPIs) showing usage and engagement, and the museum has benefited from increased exposure, ticket sales, and fan engagement.

Our interactive experiences at Graceland were game changers for the whole fan experience because there were so many different parts of the property that a visitor could see but not touch. For example, there's an entire wing of Elvis's vehicles that are protected behind velvet ropes, as are many of the rooms at Graceland. It's fascinating Elvis history, but the visitor can't get engaged. The interactive experiences that we installed for the client allowed fans to get active and involved.

OUR INTERACTIVE EXPERIENCES AT GRACELAND WERE GAME CHANGERS FOR THE WHOLE FAN EXPERIENCE.

Fans want to have that experience, like Elvis, of driving around in a golf cart, or they want to see themselves with Elvis, either being serenaded in a movie or appearing with him in a movie poster.

Graceland was a good example of us bringing together all five Ds to really mastermind and ultimately deliver a series of interactive, immersive experiences for the client. It started with **Discovery**. In that crucial first step, we asked, *What are the key values of the brand? What's the agenda? What do you want to accomplish in terms of the technology and use cases?* Next, we moved into **Design**, working closely with the client to design a series of fun, engaging experiences. Next, we moved into **Development**, assembling both the physical items, such as the golf carts, and the technical ones, like the hardware and software that powers the experiences. After that was **Deployment**, installing all the equipment on-site and beta testing the experiences. And finally, **Data**, giving the client real-time access to data on users and fan engagement.

ON THE MAT: WORKING WITH CORNELL WRESTLING

Not all projects follow such a predictable, step-by-step process. For example, another project we completed during the Covid pandemic was for the wrestling program at Cornell University. The sport of wrestling has a long and rich tradition at Cornell, and they compete at a national level, both individually and as a team. Cornell has one of the only free-standing college wrestling facilities in the nation, the Friedman Center, completed in 2002.

We got involved with the Cornell Wrestling project a bit late because most of the discovery part of the project had already been completed internally. They were in the process of completing a huge renovation of the Friedman Center, and we caught wind of the project from a large format printing company that didn't have the digital capabilities to bring new, immersive experiences to the new space. So they brought us in. The Friedman Foundation had provided a substantial new gift to completely reimagine the whole space, build a new facility, add a new player lounge, extend the gym, etc.

By the time we arrived, they had this great shiny, new construction project but not much inside the facility. We approached them and said, *Let us reimagine the environmental design of this new facility. Grant us a consulting contract, and we will design the interior of the new space, while adding some of our technical elements to simply reimagine the space for you.* Lucky for us, they agreed to do that.

In that case, there was not a lot of **Discovery**; it was more like, "Okay, let's go." We got involved from a design standpoint, where we rendered out both physical and digital elements for the new space. We designed elements such as window signage or wall art, but again, our Trojan horse has always been the digital elements, and so that's where the multimedia platform took shape. They wanted to have an attraction for not only current student wrestlers but for recruits as well.

We built out a multimedia platform that would memorialize the great history of Cornell Wrestling. Using touch screen displays, users could easily navigate through generations of Cornell Wrestling success from the 1920s to the present day. We installed a Hall of Fame feature that memorialized great Cornell wrestlers of yesteryear, with photographs and video highlights of wrestlers who had competed in the National Collegiate Athletic Association (NCAA) championships or in the Olympics.

In addition to the history part, we also added the current roster, with player profiles for each Cornell wrestler. It's like a virtual player card with a wrestler's stats, highlights, and background information. Parents, fans, and recruits love coming to matches and checking this out.

We also proposed adding an interesting feature using what's called *dimensional graphics* or *environmental graphics*. For example, on the main wall of the new facility, in large 3D letters were the words *Committed to Excellence*. We then had a projector running a highlight reel on each of those letters. What was unique about this installation was that each letter had its own piece of content. It wasn't just a flat image. Each letter was a part of the video that was playing back.

That really won the day for the project, and we were awarded a contract to move forward from **Design** into **Development** and **Deployment**. We then worked with the large format printer to produce our designs and install them in the new facility. We integrated the touch screens and built out the software platform, something we now offer as a stand-alone service to prospective clients. For example, the Cornell hockey team is now looking to do something similar.

The Cornell Wrestling installation also led directly to a new project with Stanford University. The Stanford athletic director happened to be at Cornell for the grand opening of the new, reimagined wrestling facility. When he saw it, he said, "We want this!" We are now working with Stanford Baseball on a similar interactive experience. The response by the Stanford AD was a total validation of the value we can bring to universities, museums, and other venues. It's nice to have an institution like Stanford, a storied university in the heart of Silicon Valley, the home of innovation, paying compliments to our work and eventually becoming our client.

In terms of the last step in the process, **Data**, Cornell was less concerned about usage and engagement metrics and more about having a system that they could easily update. As new student athletes enter the program, Cornell can use a back-end content management system that allows for a student athlete, admin, or intern to easily add new wrestlers to the system. They can add a bio, upload photos or highlights, then hit refresh, and the new content shows up immediately on the touch screen.

The interactive displays and other features have also become a great recruitment tool for Cornell Wrestling. As with all the Ivy League colleges, there is a lot of athletics history at Cornell. That is a part of their legacy. But when Cornell combined that historical content with modern digital elements, features that you might see at a place like Penn State or Michigan, it was a way for them to show that they were keeping pace with some of these Power Five schools. Obviously, there's a bit more nuance for Ivy League colleges, which don't allow athletic scholarships, but the new installation has been very successful for us and our client.

The Cornell Wrestling project was a good example of how we sold our design services to first envision a new space, and then got the contract to bring those design elements to fruition. There are two aspects to the design process. One, as demonstrated previously, environmental renderings create an aesthetic of a reimagined space. And two, designing the software's user interface to match that aesthetic, which completes the project holistically to have a consistent look and feel throughout.

MANAGING THROUGH COVID

We completed both the Graceland and the Cornell projects during Covid, which was not always so easy. Supply chain challenges were at their peak and even just logistic issues of being able to get on campus were a problem. One day, we drove up with a whole team from Philadelphia to Cornell's campus in Ithaca, New York, only to be told that we couldn't step foot on campus because of Covid protocols. It took a full year to complete a project that probably should have taken six months.

There were other operational challenges during that time as well. It made my job very difficult from a human resources standpoint because I needed to make sure that our team members felt comfortable and safe while working or traveling. We had to plan for things like separate car rentals or find accommodations that would make everyone feel comfortable and safe.

The pandemic affected our client installations as well. We opened our Elvis immersive experiences at Graceland while Covid was still raging. However, with so many other attractions shut down around the country, the volume of visitors expected at the museum was likely to be enormous. Masks were optional in Memphis at that point, but some visitors were likely to be more concerned about the spread of the virus than others. We were especially worried about our touch screen displays, thinking that perhaps we should hand out stylus pens rather than allowing visitors to touch the screen with their fingers. We also considered having antibacterial wipes next to each of the kiosks. We considered all those options, but in the end, the museum decided to simply keep things the way they were and to allow fans to determine what experiences they were comfortable using and how they would use them.

The Covid pandemic was nearly unprecedented when it came to sports and live events. Perhaps not since World War II had athletic events been so curtailed, especially so for professional sports. As a live-event technology company, we had to completely rethink our business. Leveraging our unique approach, we pivoted, focusing more on our services and domain expertise. We strove to commiserate with our clients and began to envision a day when things would reopen again. We were fortunate to find clients outside of our traditional wheelhouse of professional sports teams, the Elvis Presley Experience and Cornell Wrestling, who were using the pandemic to strategize and rethink their spaces. There were certainly challenges along the way, but we learned a lot during that period, and it helped to refine our best practices, which is where we turn in the next chapter.

Snapdragon / FERRARI PREMIUM PARTNER

Formula One Ferrari drivers, Charles Leclerc and Carlos Sainz, pose with themselves

A user virtually kicking a field goal inside the Washington Social Lounge

An inside look at the Columbus Blue Jackets Fan Zone

Bad investment offer

Tampa Bay Buccaneers Sales Center VR

Graceland's interactive golf cart experience and dance floor

The Coca-Cola Corner Home Run Challenge activation

Washington Social Lounge with VR Helmets

Original hand sketch of the Morphing Station and cost of metul

The first Morphing Station bobblehead prototype at NBA Jam Session in Houston

The reimaged space inside the Friedman Wrestling Center at Cornell University

The reimaged space inside the Friedman Wrestling Center at Cornell University (cont'd)

CHAPTER 6

BEST PRACTICES

ASK A LOT OF QUESTIONS

In terms of best practices, I think it all starts with the most important one: *Ask a lot of questions.* This is one of the principles that I drive home to our sales team. There is a general theory that if you're a salesperson, you must sell things. But that's not exactly right. The sales process is not just about blathering on and on about your product or service. It's really about learning the needs of the buyer. And to do that, you need to ask a lot of questions. Before we get started on any project or any concept, we try to ask as many questions as possible.

Some of this thinking comes from my own upbringing. With both of our parents working full time, my siblings and I were latchkey kids. In this summer, this meant that our parents would drop us off at our grandparents' house at about eight in the morning, and we would stay there until about six in the evening, when my mom got off work. I was very active, but at lunchtime, or when I wasn't playing outside, I would sit with my grandparents and just ask them questions.

I loved hearing their stories and learning about what it was like growing up during the Great Depression. My grandfather was a first-generation Greek immigrant, and my grandmother was second-generation Irish. She had to leave school at just fourteen to start working in a factory. Her main message to me was just to always work hard and save money. She was very frugal; saving money was very important. I remember her telling me stories about taking the bus with her girlfriend to go to New York City, just to experience life in the big city. My grandparents grew up in the Catskills, married young, moved down to the Newark area, had six kids, and eventually settled in the Toms River area near the Jersey shore. They worked hard for everything that they were able to achieve in life.

They weren't wealthy by any stretch, but for uneducated first- and second-generation immigrants, they were able to provide a comfortable life for their six kids.

Both my parents came from very big families. Growing up, I remember going to weddings all the time. That was a different era. Recently, I asked my teenage daughter how many weddings she had been to. She said maybe one. I told her that when I was her age, I went to so many family weddings that I became a wedding DJ!

My grandfather was a busy body, always doing something. He could not sit still. He had been a teamster, and he worked tirelessly. He was the type of guy that, if we were sick at school, would drive over to pick us up. If he had to wait, he would pull weeds in front of the schoolyard just to keep busy. He also instilled in me some skills I would later use at MVP Interactive. It was kind of embarrassing for a kid, but we would drive around and he would make me essentially dumpster dive in people's garbage. In the suburbs, people would put out an old couch, or a bicycle, or whatever, onto the curbside. He would drive around and have me retrieve these random pieces of garbage, and then he would go build something. As an eight-year-old, I was mortified to be rummaging through someone's trash. But then two days later, I would have a new bicycle. So it was worth it. Besides, there have been times at MVP Interactive when we have had to resort to a bit of dumpster diving ourselves.

So I think a personal characteristic of mine is that I, from a young age, became very comfortable with asking people questions. Even now, when I meet new people, I try to make it not feel like it's an interview, but I'm just so interested in others and learning about them. And so I'll ask questions all day long. That might be why I like golf so much. You can play golf with a total stranger and, after a four-hour round, learn their whole life story.

That inquisitive nature, a willingness to ask questions, has transferred over to how we assess or qualify a sales opportunity with a new client. We certainly have a set of qualifying questions that we go through with any new client, but we go well beyond that to try to understand a client's brand message and goals. Despite our business being so technically focused, we advise our clients that we don't necessarily want to shoehorn a solution just for the sake of using technology.

We take a very consultative approach when assessing a new opportunity. In many ways, this begins the discovery phase, even before we have landed the assignment. We ask a ton of questions. What are the brand values? What's the brand messaging? What is the goal of a particular campaign? That's really where we start. Based on that client feedback, we steer our creative process to determine what engagements would

> **WE DON'T NECESSARILY WANT TO SHOEHORN A SOLUTION JUST FOR THE SAKE OF USING TECHNOLOGY.**

make the most sense for the client. The needs of a financial services brand, for example, may be far different from, say, a beer brand.

WORKING WITH AFLAC: CLOSING THE GAP

We started working with Aflac, the largest provider of supplemental insurance in the United States. Everyone knows their iconic duck quacking "Aflac!" But they wanted to extend their brand messaging and reach younger consumers, especially college students. They invested heavily in sponsoring college tours, often centered around sporting events, such as football games at Historically Black Colleges and Universities (HBCUs) or, more recently, the Women's Final Four.

The key marketing message for them was "Closing the Gap." As a supplemental insurance provider, Aflac offered products that were all about closing the gaps left by traditional health insurance. As they highlight in their ads, if you are injured and can't work, health insurance may pay your medical bills, but it won't cover lost income. The immersive engagements that we proposed to them had this same theme: closing the gap. For example, for football games, we could have a virtual field goal challenge where each time you made a field goal, the goal posts would get a little bit narrower: closing the gap. Or for a virtual basketball free throw experience, we envisioned having a windmill in front of the hoop, forcing the fan to shoot in between the blades. Based on how the fan answered some quiz questions about Aflac, the windmill would spin faster or slower: closing the gap.

For us, that's the onset of a creative process to really drive home the brand messaging and values. We use that messaging and those values to develop creative concepts that make the most sense for the client. Another example from financial services is the work we have done with USAA, which we touched on in a previous chapter. The annual Army-Navy football game is rich in history, and it's all about the allegiance of your service and the historical rivalry, whether you're an Army fan or a Navy fan. We worked with the client to really learn about their brand messaging, not just for the USAA brand but for the game itself and really for the full arc of the marketing event.

For example, we developed a series of memorable historical quiz games, tailored for either the Army or the Navy. Historically, many brands thought of experiential marketing as something "nice to have." Now the trend is moving toward brands believing it's a must-have because they value what the experience can do for their target customers and for their brand. We can create something cool all day long, but we want to give value to the brand, to be value-additive to what is likely a bigger, more holistic marketing campaign. What customers are seeing on commercials or hearing on the radio should be consistent in any experiential marketing engagements we are developing for our clients.

LEARNING BEST PRACTICES FROM OUR CLIENTS

In our work with clients, we have the opportunity to collaborate with some of the best sports marketing professionals in the business, so whenever we can, we try to incorporate their best practices into our business. In terms of outbound marketing, for example, we have a very organized effort by having dedicated sales staff assigned to prospective buyers based on vertical and geography. We have salespeople selling to agencies, to sports teams, or to brands. We also have a highly automated lead generation system that can push out two thousand emails a day to a very refined subset of individuals based on job title, location, company, and other attributes. Our messaging is constantly out there.

Word of mouth has been very positive for us as well, so our reputation is extremely important. We often receive referrals from projects that we've done in the past from other brands and sports properties. One of my favorite sales experiences is when an individual from a completely different organization happens to attend an event where our technology is featured, and then they investigate the company that produced it. Eventually, they find their way to MVP Interactive. That's happened a few times for us. It's always great when your reputation can produce sales leads organically. But we also highlight our work by sending out a monthly newsletter with a feature known as "Activation of the Month."

We manage our prospects and client contacts through a system called HubSpot. Automation has been very positive for us in our email communications, our marketing efforts, and our lead generation. We also do a good job of filming and producing a case study video of everything we produce for clients. These are usually forty-five- to seventy-five-second highlight reels, promoting the piece and showing the fan interaction and the technology in a live setting. That has been great digital collateral for us.

BEST PRACTICES AND THE FIVE DS

Once we land a new project and complete the **Discovery** process, we employ best practices in **Design** as well. After digesting the client's needs, we get into our creative element. This is where the design starts to happen, where we can do creative design, environmental design, or UI/UX design of the software to really envision new immersive experiences.

It's important for our creative team to build out according to guidelines of the brand we are working with: the colors, the font types, the messaging, everything a fan might experience from a user interface perspective. We work with the client to make sure that everything is consistent with their current branding guidelines.

We then get right into the development process. We often start with hardware because that's where you find some of the longest lead times. This could involve a hybrid of hardware procurement and/or hardware production. For example, we might need to build bespoke PCs to power an activation or work with fabricators to assemble and integrate whatever hardware components are needed. Then we get into software development, where we start building the experiences. That's where it becomes both rewarding but also challenging because, especially in our early days, we were often selling a concept that had never been built before. Over time, our experience base has developed, but we still always try to push the envelope in terms of creating new, unique immersive experiences. Each brand, for example, has a different goal in mind and maybe needs/wants a different element to its activation or technology.

NO PROJECT IS COOKIE CUTTER

In a way, everything we do is 100 percent bespoke. Hardly any project is cookie cutter. And when you're in the thick of that development, it gets very arduous, challenging, and, at times, exhausting. However, the long-term benefit is that it's given us improved knowledge and understanding of technology and how past experience can parlay into new projects. Being able to build bespoke solutions, using all these different engines, techniques, or technologies, has allowed us to continue to keep pace with technology. We talked before about the need to keep up with technology hype cycles. If we were not doing augmented reality in the beginning, we would not know how to do virtual reality, and then we would not know how to do mixed reality. It's like an educational journey where, when you're in the thick of it, you may not see the long-term value because you're so focused on getting to a short-term goal. But, in hindsight, it's what kept us—and what keeps us—relevant in terms of being able to push the limits for producing experiences that have yet to be built or yet to be rolled out.

> BEING ABLE TO BUILD BESPOKE SOLUTIONS, USING ALL THESE DIFFERENT ENGINES, TECHNIQUES, OR TECHNOLOGIES, HAS ALLOWED US TO CONTINUE TO KEEP PACE WITH TECHNOLOGY.

When it comes to deployment, especially from an operational standpoint, there's a lot of value in our years of experience. Many operational factors must be considered. This was even more important early on when basic things like reliable Wi-Fi networks were not readily available. In that case, we needed to figure out how to distribute content without any bandwidth.

There were, of course, surprises along the way. For one of our first gaming wall installations, the client wanted us to affix the video screens to the cement concourse wall, which we thought was just fine because it was in an enclosed area. What we did not account for was that the bleachers rose above that particular wall. And so, when the team went through a power washing exercise to clean out the stadium seats, the water came tumbling down and blew out nine video screens.

Operationally, there are a lot of environmental factors to consider as well. Sun exposure is another one where, especially with baseball, during hot summertime games, technology such as 3D cameras or infrared sensors don't work properly when exposed to UV light. In that case, we might need to add an appropriate shelter for photo booth or video experiences. Often, we are in a semioutdoor, if not a fully outdoor, location.

Rain and snow can present their own challenges. I vividly remember a 2013 football game between the Philadelphia Eagles and the Detroit Lions. They called it the "Blizzard Bowl." It was a regular season game where about eight inches of snow fell in an hour. We had our Morphing Stations out in front of the stadium under just a very basic tent. Thankfully, we did fabricate our unit as IP rated, which means it could handle the outdoor elements. Still, ventilation, which is necessary for any electronic device, could be affected by excessive snow. We were able to run the Morphing Station until halftime, when the client finally said, "Okay, I think you guys should probably get out of here now because we're standing in a foot of snow." But from all this, we learn, and we have developed an ever-evolving checklist of all the things we need to think about, all the what ifs. Over time, those experiences turn into a competitive advantage.

DATA CAPTURE
CLOSES THE LOOP

Finally, after all that, the activation runs, and we start to capture data on usage and engagement. In many ways, data capture and analysis close the loop on the project. If we go back to discovery, we understood the client's goals and objectives upfront. Now data helps determine if we achieved those objectives. We always want to make sure that there is a seamless transaction of sharing information between the fan, the brand, and the team.

What success looks like will be different based on the goals of the team or brand. Perhaps the goal is season ticket sales, or VIP sales, or merchandise sales. Mostly, it's long-term fan and consumer engagement. Usually, the opt-ins are strong, and that's where the connection to the team or the event goes a long way. When a client thinks about extended ROI, they see that fans are not only participating in the activation at the event, but they're not opting out after the event either. This enables the brand or team to have an ongoing relationship with the fan or customer.

A fan's affinity to a particular team helps extend that relationship to a brand through our immersive experiences. A frictionless call to action and an exchange of information to participate in a cutting-edge experience creates a positive memory well beyond an event or game. For client and customer confidentiality reasons, we don't keep fan or customer data after we have passed it onto the team or brand. Still, we know anecdotally from our clients that the impact is strong and long lasting. For our part, we try to provide as much data to the client as possible. Usage, sign-ups, put-through rates, and social shares are fairly easy to track, but as we mentioned before, we also track passive, anonymous analytics, providing a bird's-eye view perspective of the overall dwell time, the attention times, and key demographics of the assembled crowd.

One of the things that doesn't surprise me anymore, but did early on, is that the usage performance is generally evenly split between male and female fans. There's this idea that sports is such a male-centric interest, but our experience and data shows it is almost evenly split in terms of attendance and participation in immersive experiences.

DO THE RIGHT THING

As I think about best practices, I also think about some of my personal principles, and one of those that I believe in strongly is extreme transparency to a fault. I have no secrets. Do the right thing, and it's always the right thing.

For many entrepreneurs, there seems to be this new "hustle culture," often promoted on social media. There's this ever-increasing "fake it till you make it" mindset. The idea is that you should just make things up and posture yourself around famous people and glamorous things until you're perceived as successful, whether you have built a great business or not. Of course, there's always a degree of "faking it" in the beginning in terms of your capabilities because everyone starts at zero, and going from zero to one requires some creativity. For us, it was having a presentation that showed these immersive concepts that didn't exist yet. But we were confident we could build them.

When you are trying to staff your company with true believers who want to be a part of your journey, being transparent often pays dividends. Maybe you don't have a lot of resources and you can't pay people the salaries they deserve. If you're a well-funded venture capital start-up, maybe that's not the case, but for most entrepreneurs trying to bootstrap their companies, that's the reality. And you need to do everything that you can to instill trust in the people that are willing to help you grow your business, knowing that they're making personal sacrifices. That starts by being fully transparent with them.

Certainly, there's some salesmanship required for any successful start-up, and to be a good salesperson, you need to be able to tell a good story. As my wife might say, I embellish stories to make a better story. But I've never resorted to misleading or lying about our capabilities to clients or prospects. It's best to be transparent, even with bad news. For example, projects, even the best-planned ones, can get delayed. Especially in the start-up world, everything is zigzag. And when you're building bespoke technology, there is certainly no straight line. On paper, you plan it all out, and then something changes. It's like Mike Tyson said: "Everyone has a plan until they get punched in the mouth."[7]

Sometimes that punch comes sooner rather than later. But we have found that the sooner we get ahead of those issues and present them to our clients with full transparency, usually the bad news isn't as bad as you think it is. If you have a reasonable client (and certainly not all of them are, but you're still better off being up front), they will understand. But if you try to hide behind the problem, if you don't disclose the issues, then it's a big surprise to them during crunch time. That's usually when things go south. And so, overall, one of our best practices, both for me personally and for the culture I have tried to instill at our company, is to be as open and transparent as possible. That's gone a long way for us.

Lying can be easy for some people, I suppose, but for me, as my mother can attest, not telling the truth has always been difficult. I

---

7   Bob Ford, "A Change of Pace for 76ers," *Philadelphia Inquirer*, June 2, 2009, D3.

recall one summer afternoon I was playing wiffle ball with my friends in the middle of the street and one of my buddies had the genius idea of spray-painting bases onto the pavement. After he tossed me a can of spray paint, I leaned down, shook the can, and proceeded to spray a square to represent first base. I knew it was wrong, but my thirteen-year-old self couldn't fight the peer pressure.

Well, nearly immediately after I put the cap back on the can, I heard the call of my mother from the front door. It wasn't a scream or a caught-you-red-handed tone; she simply asked what I was doing. I felt like I died on the inside. Feeling the heat of my face turning red, I confessed. I could not resist, and much to my surprise, she did not scold me or take out her favorite wooden spoon to hit my backside but commended my honesty despite not approving of my behavior. While not exactly George Washington cutting down the cherry tree, that moment has stayed with me ever since and it's why I firmly believe that doing the right thing will always be the right thing. Little did I know that experience would carry on into my professional life.

While working with Anheuser-Busch, arguably the world's largest sports marketing company, we had a production go awry during the start of the NFL Season. We had an activation that needed to be installed for opening day in Cincinnati, where I was responsible for operating and deploying a 360-degree green screen video device that would superimpose a fan onto midfield. Well, there was only one problem: my technical colleague, who was responsible for installing and running the software, had a personal issue in New York and missed his flight to Cincinnati. I was not aware of this fact until 6:00 a.m. on game day and we needed to be up and running by 11:00 a.m. sharp. I left my hotel with the equipment, arrived at the stadium, shook hands with my client, and proceeded to assemble the equipment as if nothing was wrong.

Shortly into assembly, I heard my mother's voice again. It was the same feeling I had as a thirteen-year-old boy and knew I had to disclose the disappointing news to our client that we could not produce this experience in time. I easily could have faked it and hacked together an experience without the client ever knowing, but I could not go against my principles. Doing the right thing is always the right thing to do. Gratefully, my client also did not take out her wooden spoon when I confessed the problem. Like my mother, she appreciated my honesty. We eventually got everything ready for the next game, and it ran smoothly for the remainder of the season.

Some best practices you learn while growing up. Others you develop over time by working in an industry for many years. Still more you might learn from other people, from either inside or outside your organization. In the end, it is those accumulated best practices that help us work with clients to envision and create engaging, new immersive experiences. But what makes an experience really "great"? That's where we turn our attention in the next chapter.

CHAPTER 7

CREATING A GREAT EXPERIENCE

THERE ARE MANY FACTORS THAT GO INTO CREATING a great immersive experience. It all starts with creating an experience that is fun, interesting, and engaging for the fan. But a truly great experience goes beyond that and is also great for the team and the brand sponsor. When all these elements come together, it's a perfect storm of greatness.

Leading brands and sports properties are increasingly linking the values of their customers to their own in what might be called values-based marketing. Marketers are realizing that customers no longer care simply about the product or service you offer but the values you espouse and, most importantly, put into practice. Increasingly, the immersive experiences we are creating for clients reflect these values.

TAKING THE HIGH ROAD

A good example of that is a project we recently completed for HiRoad Insurance, a division of State Farm. HiRoad is focused primarily on college students. You are seeing this more and more now, where a larger brand launches subbrands to target different demographic groups. This is happening in insurance, financial services, or even things like mobile phones. In the case of HiRoad, they are a health and auto insurance company that targets college students. While marketing to a younger and well-educated demographic, they are leaning in on technology to promote their brand and engage meaningfully with their demographic group. For HiRoad, we produced a fun and engaging interactive trivia game that was housed on a traveling trailer, which would go from campus to campus at different events to evangelize their brand and communicate their values.

HiRoad knew that they wanted to do a traveling campus tour around college events, but they had envisioned using more analog experiences such as typical tailgating activities like Baggo or horse-shoes. They approached us and said that their market data showed their key demographics were millennials and Generation Z, all of them tech-focused young professionals or college students. They felt that these analog experiences were not really going to tell their story and truly connect with their prospective customers. They told us they did not want anything too extravagant but something contextual so that we could learn about the participants by using technology.

We came up with an engaging memory-quiz game that would ask certain questions to help promote safer driving habits. HiRoad added a charity component to the user experience in that if the participant scored a certain point, they would donate a dollar match to a particular charity. There was an important philanthropic element to the experience. Based on market research, they had determined that younger generations showed greater compassion and assigned higher value to charitable and philanthropic activities than older generations. It was a smart way to build affinity for their brand.

The interactive quiz game was displayed on a touch screen mounted to the side of the trailer. After the event, the trailer could be folded up, hitched to the back of a truck, and driven to the next event. In addition to the quiz game on the touch screen, there was a second screen that displayed the charitable component: how much money had been donated to charity during the marketing campaign. The amount would increase in real time as the user answered more questions correctly.

The quiz-game experience was brought to all kinds of college events, from football Saturdays to Pride festivals. As usual, participants would register for the activity by providing basic demographic information such as name, school, email, etc. Based on data the client could access on MVP Live, usage and engagement for the quiz game were very strong. It's safe to say that, in general, we were getting a new user for every minute the quiz game was displayed. Typically, the activation would run for about three hours if it was available during a game but much longer if it was available at a festival, perhaps stretching over several days.

Regarding KPIs, clients are increasingly interested in "put-through" times, or how many users can participate in an experience over a given period. This has changed some in the last decade, as clients have become less interested in longer experiences. In the past, we might develop a VR experience where the user is completely immersed in the experience and forgets that they are in the real world. Now we focus more on quick hits, how to create a fun and engaging experience but one that doesn't take too long. This works for consumers as well. In a world of fifteen-second TikTok videos and 140-character Twitter posts, consumers are increasingly looking for shortened experiences.

Their mobile interactive quiz game, of course, came with the usual operational challenges. We understood that this was going to be a semioutdoor structure, meaning that it would be enclosed but it would still need to travel and be exposed to the elements to a certain degree. As I mentioned before, direct UV light can be a challenge for touch screen displays. There are outdoor solutions that can handle that, but it still helps to have it sheltered to prevent glare and high heat. That said, we can't control the position of the sun, and if it's late afternoon in Phoenix during the summer, things are going to get hot. You live and learn. Overall, however, the quiz-game experience was great, both for consumers and for the brand.

THE HOME RUN CHALLENGE AT THE COLORADO ROCKIES

Creating a great experience also means, at times, pushing the envelope in terms of technology, but that can certainly bring its own challenges as well. We have been working with the Colorado Rockies over the last five Major League Baseball (MLB) seasons. They have installed two of our gaming wall units at their baseball stadium, Coors Field. The gaming wall is a large touch screen display that provides full simulated sporting activity. For the Rockies, we created a virtual Home Run Challenge. We originally called it the *Home Run Derby*, but then I got an email from a MLB executive, on Christmas Eve no less, issuing a cease-and-desist order to stop using the phrase because they owned the rights to it. And so the "Home Run Challenge" was born.

For the user, the on-screen stadium is a replica 3D-rendered model of Coors Field. Without anything readily available on the market, we also had to build a bespoke interactive baseball bat that functions very similar to a Nintendo Wii remote. There are no wires; it's connected through Wi-Fi. The speed, velocity, and location of the users' swing would determine how well they did on the Home Run Challenge, whether it would be a pop-up, a ground out, or a home run.

These integrated wireless connected bats, of course, had to be charged overnight. I can't tell you how many phone calls we received telling us the technology wasn't working, and we would ask, "Did you charge them overnight?" Sure enough, that was usually the fix.

As I said before, environmental conditions or human error often plays a factor, because one misunderstanding could ruin someone's impression of an experience. To help address this, we make sure to create user manuals for all our interactions and also train clients on how to use and maintain the technology. It also helps to have a brand or activity ambassador on-site who can help troubleshoot any problems.

The Home Run Challenge for the Colorado Rockies was also a good example of the ultimate age-transcending experience. Whether playing T-ball, high school baseball, or even competing in the minor leagues, no matter your age or real-life batting skills, anyone can get in there and give it a try. We tweaked the technology so that it gauged the quality of your swing as opposed to simply the velocity. That way, it was able to measure skill in an enjoyable way. It was a fun home run game in which, once you got the hang of it, anyone could be an all-star.

The Home Run Challenge lives on, and we are now in our sixth season at Coors Field. It's been very popular. The Rockies not only have a sponsor for the game, but they also charge fans five dollars to participate because it's so popular. Each year, we try to add a new wrinkle to the game. This year, for example, we added a feature where a video of the user in the Home Run Challenge appears on the stadium's jumbotron. How cool is that? And, of course, that becomes a digital keepsake and can be downloaded and shared on social media. In that case, the Rockies are not too concerned with usage data. They just want to make sure fans are having a great time—indeed, a great experience.

THE IMPORTANCE OF PROJECT MANAGEMENT

Another factor in creating a great experience is how well project management is run. There are always a lot of moving parts between the client, MVP Interactive, and any outside vendors we are working with. Making sure that milestones are hit and deliverables are finished throughout the course of development is critical. In many ways, that really starts at the contract stage. There are a couple of challenges when we take on a new project. Let's say we think it's going to be a twelve-week development timetable. And the client is pressuring us to deliver in six weeks because an event date is firmly established. In that case, we need to accelerate the development process and really shoehorn all the activities into a shortened time frame, working backward from the event date to determine what and when we need to deliver. Often a real challenge is making sure that client approvals are done on time.

When we complete a user interface or design element for an interaction, we deliver it to the client. We need to give them enough time—but not too much time, depending on the schedule—to request any changes, before moving on to the next ticket item. Procuring hardware, dealing with supply chain issues, or managing fabrication: all these moving parts play into the chronology of the development cycle. Software development is another key deliverable, often in parallel with our other activities. We are building alpha builds, then beta builds, and finally testing for software crashes or bugs.

MAKING SURE THAT MILESTONES ARE HIT AND DELIVERABLES ARE FINISHED THROUGHOUT THE COURSE OF DEVELOPMENT IS CRITICAL.

Normally, AAA gaming studios take years to do that. Often, we must condense that workflow into just weeks. It's certainly not normal or industry standard. Over time, we have developed a unique ability to deploy bespoke technology rapidly.

THE COCA-COLA CORNER

For just about every project, it seems we are working under the gun. One example is when we launched our first version of the virtual home run game for the New York Mets in 2016. Citi Field had just gone through a sponsorship change—a fact of life in the sports business—moving from Pepsi to Coca-Cola. The "Pepsi Porch" was to become the "Coca-Cola Corner," an upper-deck entertainment zone for fans. We worked with the new beverage sponsor, who wanted the Coca-Cola Corner to be a real party zone, with a DJ and concessions. It was to be outfitted with lounges, chairs, couches, along with fun games like Baggo. It was like baseball's version of an upper-deck tailgate party.

Of course, Coca-Cola also wanted something more technically driven and tailored to baseball. We proposed a virtual home run game, and they said, "Great!" First, we fabricated a batting cage enclosure for our gaming wall unit that would also include some storage space. There would be three different virtual batting stations. It was also our first iteration of creating these connected, wireless bats. We partnered with a touch screen provider for our displays and then built the three-foot-by-three-foot video wall inside an enclosure. Today, you can do all that on a single large ninety-eight-inch display screen, like the gaming wall units the Rockies use. But back then, you needed nine different screens to achieve the same thing.

We were on a very tight time schedule and were working on the installation nearly nonstop for four or five days before Opening Day. And while Opening Day is big anywhere, it's especially big on one of the world's biggest stages in New York. It was not until two days before Opening Day that the screens finally arrived on a pickup truck at Citi Field. We installed them in the enclosures and got them connected and wired. Suddenly, we wondered, *Where's the control box for the screens?*

When you connect nine different video screens, you need a central brain, called the control box, that networks all those screens together and feeds them into a computer. We asked our screen vendor about the control box, and they said, "It's back at our office in Pittsburgh." We had less than thirty-six hours until the opening of the gates. By that time, it was ten o'clock at night and too late for next-day shipping. But our vendor got someone (God bless him!) from the office to load the control box in their car and drive all night to get to New York in the morning.

That was not the last issue. The wireless bats were not ready either. We had found some high-density foam bats from a third-party supplier. We have since moved to producing our own bats using a sturdier plastic, but this was our first iteration of the installation. We sawed off the handles of the foam bats and then hollowed them out to provide room for the internal electronics. Using a 3D printer, we then fabricated a plastic enclosure for all the electronic components and batteries. That way, they would fit tightly and securely into the handle. Then we built a collar that allowed the handle to be screwed back into the barrel of the bat. This was all done by hand.

We did not have enough time to commercially fabricate the 3D-printed plastic enclosures, so we had to bring a 3D printer on-site to Citi Field. We thought we would work through the night to produce six enclosures for six bats to be ready by game time. But then suddenly, at 8:00 p.m., the stadium went completely dark. All the power was automatically shut off each night, and the only rooms that had electricity were the restrooms.

We stayed up through the night working in the men's bathroom to 3D print the enclosures. When we finally had all the bats ready, the sun was coming up over Queens. In late March or early April, Opening Day in New York City is often not a warm opening day. On this day, it was howling winds and brutally cold. With the bats assembled, we still needed to network them to the game and then connect everything to the internet. Everything had to proceed in sequence. Even our software development could not be completed until the bats were fully assembled. It's all congruent and each step must proceed in lockstep with the other. Finally, at about 10:50 a.m., everything was tested and ready. The gates were opening in ten minutes. Somehow, we got Opening Day off without a hitch. That was a very popular activation that ran for multiple seasons.

Admittedly, our project management process probably wasn't as tight as it should have been, and we've improved it over time. But the schedule is always tight, and there are always unforeseen issues. If there's one mishap in the supply chain, it has a domino effect on everything else. You must build buffers into your plan to account for the unexpected.

THE IMPORTANCE OF STAFFING

Another aspect of creating a great experience is having a good staffing plan, especially for on-site assistance and troubleshooting. Interns can be helpful in a couple of ways. One is by serving as on-site champions for the experience, modern-day yard barkers helping people lose that apprehension about trying something new. At times, the intern steps in themselves to get things started. Generally, when someone goes first, others will follow. It's an amazing case study in human psychology where if you have one user participate with something, the crowds soon follow. When you have a brand ambassador or an intern either calling people over or participating with the experience to kind of draw people in, that's a very clever way to drive interaction.

Good staffing should not be understated, and having someone help manage traffic around what might be a small footprint is important, because no one likes lines. People will wait in lines when they value the experience or are intrigued with a new game, but you also need to make sure that there's no blockage of the concourse. We were at the NBA All-Star game in New Orleans, where we had our bobblehead Morphing Station set up on the concourse. This is where the NBA had designated as their sponsor entitlement location. But it was maybe ten to fifteen feet from a concession area, and the Smoothie King Arena in New Orleans has a very narrow concourse. The activation became so popular that it created a fire hazard because people were lined up and blocking the natural egress of the concourse. We needed to put up stanchions to separate our line from the concession line. It started to look like people lining up for TSA at the airport. Those are the types of operational issues that have nothing to do with technology. It's the human behavior factor that you need to consider when you're activating new engagements.

But technology issues crop up as well. When a fan participates in an immersive experience, the speed in which they receive their takeaway is important. You don't want someone to wait two days after an event to receive their photo or video. Sometimes, that's completely out of our control in that perhaps the facility does not have reliable internet or bandwidth to push out content at high volume. Often, we do our own checks and balances and, if necessary, build our own network. We can even build experiences that can be run offline. If we lose internet, the experience still runs, and a backup server archives the email messages. It could be a few minutes or, worst case, a few hours before things come back online, and then we can push that content out to the users.

COMBINING THE IMMERSIVE WITH THE PHYSICAL

Another way to create a great experience is to pair an interactive, immersive experience with a physical keepsake to take with you. At the NBA game in New Orleans, we had our bobblehead Morphing Station, but we also attached it to a printer so that the fan could take a printed copy of the image with them. In addition to the digital version that they could download or share online, they got a real memento as a takeaway, a branded All-Star weekend photo of their bobblehead. It proved to be incredibly popular. Fans would take one photo and customize it with different hair pieces and jerseys and then get back in line because they wanted to go home with five different photos. After all, it was free.

As a call to action, free remains undefeated. I give a lot of credit to the brands that are underwriting these experiences. It's valuable to the customer because not only do they get their hands on unique technology, but they also get to participate in something firsthand. And, unlike most things in this world, it's absolutely free. When you have a call to action with no friction, it helps drive the experience. That's what leads to a cherished memory and provides a long-lasting positive impression.

Leading sports teams and venues are recognizing the need to create great immersive experiences that are complementary to the action on the court, diamond, or field. They recognize that the total cost of attending a sporting event is only going up and up, between ticket prices, parking, concessions, and gear. They recognize that they need to provide more value for the fan's hard-earned dollar. I was recently attending the National Sports Forum in Los Angeles, and the biggest takeaway when it comes to sponsored activation is it's no longer a nice-to-have; it's a must-have. Creating a valuable game-day experience is paramount to what teams are focused on. Working hand in hand with sponsors and technologists like us, they are bringing these immersive engagements to their fans.

THE 3252 AND THE LOS ANGELES FOOTBALL CLUB

The Los Angeles Football Club (LAFC), one of the newer Major League Soccer franchises, is a good example of a team that is creating a valuable game-day experience for fans. They are doing this by promoting the traditional culture of the soccer fan base. LAFC has created a supporter's club where the number one rule for the fans is to be as rowdy, as loud, and as fun as possible. It's become a movement. All their different supporter groups have been assembled into an umbrella organization called the 3252. Not only do they support the team in the stadium on game day, but they also get involved in community building projects around Los Angeles. It's taking sport and community involvement to a whole new level.

These are all the elements of creating a great experience for the fan and even for the community. For their part, advertisers are embracing this new form of experiential marketing. I discussed above how immersive experiences can eliminate that friction that might be caused by a traditional hard solicitation. When brands get involved in creating these immersive experiences, there's no apprehension on the part of the user to participate with a brand experience.

If you look overseas, particularly in England with the Premier League, there is a culture that is very much antiadvertising. It's not the same consumer-based market that exists in the United States, but we are increasingly moving in that direction. What's valuable for advertisers and sponsors that are doing these activations is owning an experience through technology.

On the surface, the brand is secondary to the experience, but more broadly, whether it's more subliminal or more active through solicitation afterward, the affinity to that experience is now going to create a better relationship with the consumer. When a fan participates in any of these experiences, it's building something that is memorable. The fan always has that memory, one that is

> NEVER UNDER-ESTIMATE THE IRRATIONAL PASSION OF A SPORTS FAN.

forever tied to a brand. The next time you hear that Coca-Cola jingle, it's like, "Oh, I remember the Coca-Cola Corner!" Or "I remember the USAA fan event at the Army-Navy game. That was awesome that they produced that. I want to be a client because they value the same thing that I value."

Never underestimate the irrational passion of a sports fan. The brand affinity of the team tied to the sponsor goes a long way. I catch myself doing it as well, even as a business owner. I'm a season ticket holder with the Philadelphia Eagles. I was at the stadium and saw Firstrust Bank, and it's like, "Hey, season ticket holders get a 4 percent yield on their savings account." That's much better than my current rate. And I'm like, "That's awesome. Maybe I'll get an Eagles credit card too. I'm in."

Immersive experiences can help ease the relationship between a brand and its customers, as compared to traditional advertising, which can feel like you are being hit over the head. It's more of a natural, holistic relationship, where you are learning about a brand or tying a commonality of the team or the sport with the relationship to the brand. For the consumer, it's very powerful to be drawn to a new experience. The more participants and the more exposure that fans have to these sponsored activations, the easier it's going to be for the brand to convert that user into a consumer.

And because everything is done through data and is digitally distributed, the consumer and the brand are connected. It's an easy exchange of information for a unique experience, and it costs nothing. The brand can then solicit the fan and promote their products and services until they opt out or become a client. That's the reason why brands spend millions of dollars to be sponsors throughout sports and entertainment and why they are increasingly looking to deploy immersive engagements. It's all about creating a great experience.

CHAPTER 8

DEVELOP THE RIGHT TEAM

THERE'S NO QUESTION THAT CREATING GREAT EXPE-
riences for teams, brands, and fans starts with developing the
right team.

For any early-stage technology or creative company, it all begins
with having an MVP. Not a "most valuable player," but a "minimally
viable product." In my case, I was just running with an idea, a concept.
There were no reference materials to use when pitching the vision for
the business. That added a unique challenge for us. Still, I felt that
being the first to market was going to be our competitive advantage.
But that is not always the case because there's no benchmark, no
North Star to guide you. Many entrepreneurs get fixated on an idea
simply because they think it's a good idea. They then try to execute on
that idea. But without a market need, you really don't have a solution.

Fortunately for us, that wasn't necessarily the case. We knew that
teams and brands were looking for innovative ways to engage with
their fans. But, in many ways we were still ahead of the market. The
appetite wasn't necessarily established yet for this type of immersive
experience. We were a step ahead in terms of experiential marketing,
whereas brands and teams were just starting to value these new
approaches. Selling vision and ideas is always a challenge. As a founder,
your passion and drive—even your naivete—can get you pretty far,
but only so far.

GREAT DESIGN STARTS WITH
A GREAT GRAPHIC DESIGNER

I realized early on that we needed to translate our vision and ideas into
something tangible, or at least something you could see, if perhaps
not experience just yet. To that end, one of my first key hires was a
graphic designer, Gavin Renwick, who was someone who could turn

concepts into visual renderings. But even before that important task, I wanted him to improve the creative marketing of our new company. Our first website was little more than a landing page, but it looked slick and professional. I went so far as to add NFL, MLB, NBA, and other league logos on our website, until I got a call from one of the league lawyers, who said, "I don't think we actually work together." *Work together* yet, I thought, but I took down the logos.

In those early days, a good graphic designer like Gavin was critical for giving the customer a tangible view of what this new, immersive experience could look like. We were working on a pitch for the video game maker Angry Birds, one that involved using facial-morphing technology. This was well before the days of Snapchat and modern iPhones, which put face filters at your fingertips. Angry Birds was working with an NFL team, and we pitched them on having a Morphing Station, where fans could take their image and morph it into one of the Angry Birds.

We wanted to show the customer what the output was going to look like and to demonstrate that it would be of high quality. But it was very difficult to render that concept because designers had no experience with facial restructuring. We spent a considerable amount of time developing mock-ups so that the client could see how much fun it could be for football fans to morph themselves into one of the Angry Birds. Ultimately, we did not end up working with the client, but it was a good lesson for us, and it laid the groundwork to pitch other character-morphing concepts as well.

That led to our first project with the NBA Jam Session, as I discussed above. After we presented this bobblehead concept, we needed to show the client what the user experience was going to look like. But we did not have a lot to work with. We bought some cheap bobbleheads and took pictures of the figures. Then, we found some 3D models of Lego characters with hair, but we still needed to figure out how to apply a plastic face filter over the user's face so they would match the texture of the bobblehead body. That required a fair amount of R&D to compile and produce the rendering and show it to the client. We also needed to make sure that we could deliver the product. A great designer can translate a concept into a compelling rendering, but you need a great development team to bring it to reality, and we were able to do that for the NBA. Looking back at those early Morphing Stations, I almost cringe because our capabilities have improved so much since then and our output is now of much higher quality. Proudly, our designer, Gavin Renwick, has not only grown into representing our design elements in step with technology but is now the creative director of MVP Interactive.

GETTING OUR FIRST SALESPERSON

As I started to grow the company, I knew I needed help in the sales area. When you are CEO of a start-up, you are the "C" of everything. You wear a lot of hats, and on any one day, I might have on my sales hat, my design hat, my finance hat, my put-things-together-with-glue hat, and on and on. But having a great salesperson, especially one who is as passionate as you are, can really help take the company to the next level. As an entrepreneur, when you can play into the passion point of an individual, one who really believes in the product, the vision, the company, and who aligns culturally with you as the leader, that's something you can really leverage. But finding a good salesperson who can articulate the vision as well as you, who can get in front of the right people, and who is also willing to work strictly on commission is certainly challenging.

I was cautious at first about hiring an outside salesperson. I was doing most of the sales myself. When I was introduced to an early salesperson, Billy Bellatty, I kind of shut him down because I felt we weren't quite ready for that yet. But he did such a fascinating job of being persistent without being annoying. I started to think that is precisely the skill you're looking for in a salesperson, someone who opens, qualifies, and ultimately closes sales opportunities without being too pushy. I've come to call it "pleasant persistence." I decided to take a flyer and bring Billy on board.

It was a big gamble for him as well because I couldn't give him an annual salary; the upside was all in commissions. But Billy was excited and enthusiastic about the addressable market, along with having the chance to work at the intersection of sports, marketing, and advertising. He had been a successful salesperson before and felt confident that he could make some waves. Still, it took time. Three months, four months, even six months went by without any closed sales. I had a conversation with him where he just said, "I've never experienced this. I've always produced in sales." I just promised him that it was going to work out, based on how everything was taking shape in our market.

As a leader, it's important to share the vision and keep up the motivation and energy to a level where people can see through the hard times to a day when they're going to be successful. And sure enough, it was just a matter of time before things started to break his way, and I'm proud to say it's been ten years and Billy is still with me. He's crushing it now and has really solidified himself as a senior leader at the company with duties well beyond the sales capacity as our managing director.

> AS A LEADER, IT'S IMPORTANT TO SHARE THE VISION AND KEEP UP THE MOTIVATION AND ENERGY.

In those early days, I had former colleagues who would catch wind of what we were building. They would approach me and say, "Hey, how can I help? I want to be a part of this." As we talked about in the previous chapter, being transparent and honest is critical. I was always very open and would say, "That's great. I would love to have you. But I can't pay you."

That's when we would come up with creative solutions. Perhaps the new candidate could start on a part-time basis, working nights or weekends, while they still held on to their full-time job. Or maybe they could work on a contract basis for a particular project. I would get creative in other ways as well. Once, I paid a new employee's rent for several months. I was also always very generous with sharing equity in the form of stock options. My attitude was "Let's all succeed together." It's like that old adage: "Would you rather own 100 percent of nothing or 10 percent of something really valuable?"

HIRING TECHNICAL TALENT

Hiring technical talent is one of the biggest challenges for a start-up. In our case, it was even more challenging because immersive technology was so new. Not many people had experience building and deploying immersive experiences. I was reluctant to hire an outside firm who might promise the world but fail to deliver. I knew I needed someone in-house. I found an old technical colleague of mine who agreed to come on board. I had to depend on his skill set dramatically to make my vision come to life, but there were many sleepless nights with building that first prototype for the Morphing Station because I felt so dependent on an individual whom I was not sure could deliver. That was risky.

During those early days, I felt that some of our challenges were acceptable because of my ignorance of not knowing how to produce or assemble the technology. In my case, I also felt a bit oversold on his capabilities, but I didn't realize that until well into the relationship. At that point, it seemed like we were making things more difficult than they needed to be. And then, when you have a personal relationship and a friendship, that presents a very challenging situation. Of course, in the technical world, or any world, ego can really get in the way of success and growth, whether my ego or someone else's. It was a lesson for me because anytime you feel completely dependent on an individual, that's a red flag. Over time, we have learned to never establish a complete dependence on any one individual, but rather to work together collectively as a team to get projects completed successfully on time and on budget.

For me it was helpful to dive into the trenches, as it forced me to immerse myself in the technical development of a project. It was very much learning by doing, and it was always all hands on deck. In many ways, that was the culture we built, where everyone lends a hand; whether from the graphic design team or the client-services team, everyone chips in.

I didn't realize in the moment why working in the trenches was so important, so helpful. Eventually, you start to realize how everything is sort of tied together. For us, being collaborative, being open, and taking a hands-on approach was very helpful. I did not fully realize that the education I was getting would be tremendously valuable in a year or two. Being hands-on in the hardware technical development process was incredibly helpful for me as well. It was an area where I could lend some knowledge and skills. Software development was a bit different because I was not a programmer.

Offshore software development can be a great way for early-stage companies to build new technology and certainly far cheaper than onshore. But again, there is a risk of overdependency. Every firm you look at is going to have a great portfolio. They can demonstrate the projects they have worked on. But there's no way to really dig into their code and evaluate how they are as programmers, what methodologies they use, or how well they can execute according to a timeline.

Those early days were very challenging because we would contract with a software developer and then halfway through the project, we had to abort and find a new developer because the development wasn't progressing according to the timeline. Eventually, we moved away from broad software development to a more targeted approach. Rather than looking for a general contractor who would oversee the entire project, we would instead serve as the general contractor and look for subcontractors with specific, niche technical skillsets. Over time, we have built a network and a community of creative technologists and software developers that we can depend on.

PROJECT MANAGEMENT IS CRITICAL

Successful technology deployment is not possible without excellent project management. The ability to define clear deliverables, set up a timeline and budget, manage internal and external resources, and deal with the innumerable challenges along the way is a treasured skillset for a company like ours. Talented project managers are hard to find, as they are very structured and well-organized individuals. Early on, I was fortunate that one of those people who heard about what we were doing and knocked on my door was Ann Marshall, a former colleague whom I had worked with before. Fortunately, she was in a financial situation where she was able to cover her expenses without earning a salary, and she just wanted to have a seat at the table.

Because I'm very collaborative by nature, I believe good ideas can come from anywhere and I try to operate with as little ego as possible.

126

So having her really manage projects both in terms of the technical bird-dogging and then also the client servicing was critical. She did an amazing job corralling all the moving parts and making sure projects were completed on time and on budget. She eventually moved on to join a larger agency, but her contribution was enormous.

I'm tremendously grateful for the colleagues that have stayed with us for the long term, when our culture aligns with their values and when the company provides and satiates what they are looking for. But I don't expect that to be everyone. I understand that each person has their own personal goals and career path. If I can have someone for two years or more, I feel like I've succeeded in creating a comfortable, valuable, and rewarding employment experience. I'm always prepared that you must anticipate some level of employee churn.

HIRING BY DATA AND BY INSTINCT

My philosophy is "Hire the athlete, not the quarterback." This is especially true when it comes to project management. We're one of about five companies that do what we do, so we do not have a big pool of experienced hires to draw from. We're not accountants or attorneys. Instead, I look to hire a personality. During the interview process, we ask a series of questions, face-to-face, to get an idea of not just their career experience but more broadly what they've done in their lives: What was their college experience like? Did they have a part-time job? What activities or organizations were they involved in? The key to asking these types of questions is to see how their past behaviors will translate into future skills. Former athletes, for example, tend to have a personality that overachieves, handles rejection well, and has a personal drive to succeed at the task at hand. Those inherent characteristics can carry over to a myriad of job titles, whether it be sales or project management.

But it really comes down to finding that right personality trait. We use something called the Kolbe A™ Index, which is a performance personality assessment. It's not a quiz; there's no wrong answers. It goes through a series of questions, first for the employer and then for the prospective employee. As the employer, you create a profile of the job and then define the main set of tasks and skills required. Through a series of questions, you establish the type of behaviors that would allow for this position to be successful. Then, as applicants come through, they also answer a series of questions that assesses them for the requirements of the job. We don't use the Kolbe A™ Index exclusively. We also use our own instinctual assessment. But if we meet someone, like them, and feel they would be a good cultural fit, we then look at the Kolbe A™ Index to see if those numbers align. If they do, we have a pretty good idea that in terms of culture, personality, and skills, they are going to succeed in that role.

That data-driven and instinctual hiring strategy has been successful for us. For example, we have been very lucky with our project management and client-services hires. It's kind of a hybrid role. For us, it's really about hiring a personality and then finding an individual who has an interest in our work and the role and who also has an inherent ability to handle different circumstances and situations. We have used this approach successfully in other roles as well, including sales, creative, technology, and product management.

LEARNING FROM SPORTS TEAMS

I've learned a lot about developing the right team from working with top professional sports teams, both on the field and in the front office. One thing that I have realized in working with sports teams is that whether you're a $100,000 business or a $1 billion business, the principles are still the same. The only difference is the number of zeros. It was an eye-opening experience for me as an entrepreneur to realize that these billion-dollar sports teams were dealing with the same challenges I was, perhaps not at the same level or scale, but similar, whether it was a personnel conflict or operational issues. As just one example, we walked into a brand-new billion-dollar sports stadium that seats seventy thousand fans only to discover that there was no power in a whole section of the building. We asked ourselves, "Who's the engineer who forgot that?"

When you're intimately involved with sports organizations, you realize that everyone deals with the same issues, the same problems, and some deal with them better than others. And from what I've experienced, it really does come down from the ownership level. As I mentioned previously, one vice president told me in confidence that some of these old-school owners treat these teams like they're billionaire toy trains. It's a hobby business, one that may or may not make money, sometimes driven by ego rather than business or team support. That certainly is starting to change, as an increasing number of savvy owners are bringing a higher level of commitment and professionalism to the management of pro sports teams.

IF YOU LOOK AT THE SPORTS ORGANIZATIONS THAT HAVE BEEN SUCCESSFUL, YOU'LL SEE THERE'S A REASON FOR IT.

If you look at the sports organizations that have been successful, you'll see there's a reason for it. There's no guarantee with the performance on the field. But if you look at where teams are at in terms of what they're doing in the community, or how they're represented in the media, or really the full arc of their ownership story, it is usually a pretty good indicator of how rock solid the organization is. On the other hand, if these same values don't stem from the ownership level, then you see issues arise, like the recent Washington Commanders scandal.

The Columbus Blue Jackets, a National Hockey League (NHL) expansion team, for example, have been successful in many ways, if not necessarily on the ice. It's a newer franchise, having recently celebrated its twentieth anniversary. They do well in terms of selling tickets and with community outreach, despite a relatively poor track record of wins and losses. They take a very strategic and somewhat conservative approach to how they take on projects, what they do in the facility, or how they conduct community outreach. That conservative, thoughtful approach has kept them in a positive-revenue-generating environment and built a high level of loyalty among the local Columbus community. They routinely sell out games, even though the fans know that they might not win, at least initially.

Working with the Blue Jackets and witnessing their approach in terms of how they choose partners or vendors makes you appreciate how those values come from the top down. Anyone associated with the Blue Jackets organization feels like they are treated like a true partner. We saw this firsthand in terms of how we won our first request for proposal for their new fan zone. They were looking for a level of commitment that was not tied to an immediate financial agreement. They appreciated the efforts we made in good faith to develop ideas for the new fan zone, which we viewed as an upfront investment and simply the cost of doing business. That commitment really resonated with them. Also, our transparent communication, the concessions we made, and the honest conversations we had with them really helped us win the project. The Blue Jackets didn't see the contract as simply a financial transaction. They came to appreciate that we cared as much about the fan zone as they did and that we were there for the long term. It was not a one-off transaction.

LESSONS FROM "FLOWER POWER" NICK

I also draw inspiration on how to develop the right team from coaches on the field. Although we rarely work directly with them—and sometimes we annoy them by interrupting practices or games—I'm a fan like anyone else, and I follow coaching decisions closely. When Nick Sirianni was announced as the new head coach of the Eagles in January 2021, he was not even forty years old, one of the youngest coaches in the league. Some fans thought his youth was an advantage in terms of being a players' coach, but others thought it meant a lack of experience. But what I've seen from him, and what I've heard about him, is that he has built a culture of transparency and a sense of accountability that everyone in the organization has toward each other.

Some thought Sirianni was a bit quirky when he first arrived in Philadelphia. In an early press conference, he used an analogy where he said that building a championship football team was like growing a flower. First you get the soil right and plant the seed. You might not see what's happening underneath the surface, but the seed is growing and roots are being formed. Over time, the seed sprouts into a plant, and eventually it blooms into a beautiful flower. This was not typical talk from an NFL football coach, especially in a tough town like Philly. He was roasted in the media as "Flower Power" Nick. But it resonated with me. I loved it. I could see similarities to building our business: planting the seed, tending it, and then watching it grow. It didn't take long for Sirianni's flower to bloom. In just his second season, he led the Eagles to a 14–3 record, a National Football Conference championship, and a trip to the Super Bowl.

SNAPDRAGON, FERRARI, AND FORMULA ONE

Developing the right team leads to great experiences for fans, brands, and teams. A good example is when we recently had the opportunity to work on one of our first international projects for Ferrari's Formula One team. The brand partner was Qualcomm's Snapdragon, which makes advanced processors and chips for smartphones, laptops, and VR devices. We were introduced to Snapdragon via their advertising agency, CAA. We have now worked on several projects with this leading advertising agency, and it's great working with them because when they bring us into new opportunities, they introduce us to the client and then kind of back away because we're a trusted partner. In some cases, agencies can be very guarded about their clients, keeping us behind the curtain, and are not always the most honest or open about disclosing to the client who is responsible for what deliverables. But over the years we have established a very positive relationship with CAA. They trust that we are going to produce, and so we gain full access to the client.

In this case, we were working with the Ferrari Formula One driving team and the Snapdragon brand to develop a "Pose with the Driver" immersive experience. We would create a photo booth engagement for what's called the "paddock," a mobile fan zone that travels to all the Formula One races around the world. Fans could walk into the unit, touch the screen on the photo booth, pose with the drivers using augmented reality, and then have the photo sent to their email.

This was a perfect example of how project management is so vital to the success of a project. We had hired a brand-new project management coordinator who had no experience in our world. She was a graduate student, fresh out of school, and had only worked in publishing. But she had just this gusto about her, almost an overconfidence in how comfortable she was to be in a new situation. I really liked that during our interview process.

We were in a very busy period with a lot of productions going on, so I was very honest and open, telling her, "Hey, you're going to get thrown in the fire here. I'm not looking for you to be an expert in anything. Just keep everything organized and help corral everyone, because we have an international team in a lot of different time zones. Managing the communication will be extremely valuable." She did an incredible job. In her first thirty days on the job, we were able to schedule very detailed weekly and biweekly meetings and make sure that all communications, milestones, and deliverables were coordinated for a successful implementation.

Working with a great partner like Snapdragon was certainly helpful as well. Their project lead was very detail oriented and, as I told the team, we learned a lot from each other. We had to follow certain principles that they used, such as how they organized their meetings or handled follow-ups. We were able to learn from them because they were such a polished group from a project management standpoint.

Procurement and logistics were also a challenge. The required hardware needed to be shipped internationally because the beta launch of the activation was going to be at a big conference in Berlin. Meanwhile, many of our vendor partners or fabrication partners were still dealing with supply chain issues related to Covid. Metal kiosks that were normally produced in four weeks were taking twelve weeks. And the schedule could not slip; we had a hard-and-fast launch date. We had to get smart quickly and work together collectively. Everyone really took on the responsibility to say, "Okay, I may be a software developer, but I'm going to do some research to see if I can find another kiosk provider." Through effective project management, we collectively pulled together our network to organize the production and delivery of all the required equipment on time.

I got the best deal out of the gig in that I got to fly out to Maranella in Italy to stay at the Ferrari campus, home to its corporate headquarters and factory. The company has their own little community, a microcosm of a city, with apartments, hotels, restaurants, and shops. Meanwhile, test tracks crisscross the landscape, and you can hear engines roaring and tires skidding. There are two hotels at opposite ends of the campus, and when you walk out of the hotel, you are smelling gasoline and burnt rubber. A pathway from the hotel leads into a town center with apartments, bars, and restaurants. Residents, most of whom work at Ferrari, have the company's flag flying from their windows. They love Ferrari that much. There is also the Ferrari Museum, and you can even rent cars and race them around the track. What Graceland is for Elvis, Maranella is for Ferrari.

The campaign was a smashing success. Someone from the Ferrari marketing team filmed the two drivers doing the experience posing with themselves, and it went viral on TikTok. Fans were clamoring to get in whenever the mobile paddock turned up at a Formula One race for the 2022 race season. We also worked with Snapdragon to produce the experience on a mobile phone. When we first photographed the drivers, we did it in a way that would make it look like a selfie, so that the on-site experience would better translate to mobile. Ferrari and Snapdragon wanted to scale the experience beyond the races, so by using webAR (web-based augmented reality) technology, we created the same experience on user's phones. That experience for Formula One has now led to a new activation we are now building for Major League Baseball and the Boston Red Sox. When you develop the right team, good things follow.

CHAPTER 9

HIGH FIVES AND HUGS

THE FAN ENGAGEMENT ECOSYSTEM

One advantage of building immersive experiences for sports teams is that we get to interface with some of the most innovative companies in the broader field of sports technology. There is now a large and growing ecosystem of sports technology providers, many of them focused on fan engagement. As I mentioned earlier, leading sports teams and brands are leveraging technology to interface with fans from the moment they buy a ticket to the game-day experience to postgame interaction. While there are many players in this emerging field, I will mention a few that are doing some cutting-edge work.

Fancam was founded in 2010 by Tinus le Roux and James Taylor (not the singer) and describes itself as a "global leader in gigapixel event photography." The word *gigapixel* means that it takes photographs of packed sports stadiums that are so precise, you can zoom in and see clear images of every single fan. Fans can then log in to Fancam, view a photograph of them and their family or friends at the game and then get a branded digital postcard that they can share on social media. It proved hugely popular, and they have photographed over three thousand events worldwide.

Realizing that these photographs, and eventually video, gave incredibly detailed views of both fan demographics and fan behavior, the company launched CrowdIQ to harness this data for the benefit of teams. CrowdIQ is quick to point out that while it uses fan photography and video, it never uses facial recognition. Savvy sports teams are now using CrowdIQ to better understand the demographics of their fan base and how that might change based on the day and time of the game. An NFL football team, for instance, might see that night games skew younger and more female while day games attract more families. They can then better tailor both their marketing and their game-day activations to the audiences they are trying to attract.

Every sports team, along with their brand sponsors, wants to increase the social media impact of live events. The more fans or members of the media who are posting about the event, the more brand value they are generating for the team and the brand. Founded by Ali Reza Manouchehri, Zoomph is a company that helps sports teams measure and amplify their social media impact. By collecting both team- and fan-generated social media posts, Zoomph provides a 360 degree view of social media performance on every platform. This can then be used to shape future content and report back to brand partners.

> EVERY SPORTS TEAM, ALONG WITH THEIR BRAND SPONSORS, WANTS TO INCREASE THE SOCIAL MEDIA IMPACT OF LIVE EVENTS.

As game day approaches for any pro or college sports team, they are typically met with a growing flood of calls or email inquiries from fans. *Are tickets still available? Where do I park?* While some of this information might be available online, many fans still call the ticket office, which can hardly field enough staff to handle all the incoming inquiries. Satisfi Labs uses AI to create chatbots for teams and leagues to answer basic questions for fans so that the call center personnel can be more productive and focus on higher-end activities, such as selling season tickets or luxury packages.

While everyone has dealt with a chatbot that was less than helpful, AI technology is evolving so fast that users are having a harder time distinguishing between bot and human. Founded by Don White and

Randy Newman (also not the singer), Satisfi Labs also collects data on fan inquiries, which can help marketing efforts and upgrade the website to provide better information. Well-designed chatbots can lead to ticket and even merchandise purchases and lead to much-improved customer service.

Leading sports teams increasingly want to move toward one-to-one marketing with fans, moving beyond broad demographic categories to better understand each fan's unique interests and needs. Tradable Bits is a company that helps them do this. Fan data can come from many sources, including ticketing systems, surveys, merchandise purchases, email or chatbot inquiries, and our on-site activations. Tradable Bits helps centralize all this data into one unified fan profile, helping teams better understand their fans and build a cohesive and comprehensive fan engagement strategy.

Austria-based Axess AG is a company that works literally on the front lines of sporting events, building and deploying secure turnstiles to scan tickets for sporting and other events. This is no small issue for sports teams. There was a major incident at a Champions League soccer game last year in France where thousands of Liverpool fans were delayed in getting into the stadium. Inevitably, especially at pro and college football teams, there is a rush to the stadium after tailgating. Stadiums need secure and efficient ways to process thousands of incoming fans quickly, and Axess AG is developing innovative gate technology to do this more effectively and efficiently. Once again, the data capture on when fans arrive at the venue can be important for marketing and fan engagement. Early arriving fans, for instance, are more likely to take advantage of food, beverage, and other engagements before the action begins.

Founded by Josh Decker in 2012, Tagboard leverages on-site screens such as the jumbotron to create interactive fan experiences using hashtags. For example, at the 2021 Goodyear Cotton Bowl, Tagboard created a hashtag competition between the two competing colleges, Cincinnati versus Alabama. Nothing gets fans going like some friendly competition, and thousands of fans were soon posting furiously using the designated hashtag to make sure their team came out on top, regardless of what was happening on the field. Fans can also use designated hashtags to have their game photos or comments posted on the jumbotron for all the crowd to see. Tagboard is showing that even the jumbotron, which was at one point just about the only technology in the stadium, can be adapted for a new socially connected world.

If you have been to an NHL hockey game recently, you may have seen some incredible imagery on the ice before the game and not just the players warming up. Quince Imaging has been a pioneer in this space for over a decade. Before a recent hockey matchup between the Vegas Golden Knights and the Seattle Kraken (two NHL teams that didn't exist ten years ago), the Golden Knight mascot skated onto the ice with sword and shield in hand, when suddenly the ice collapsed and a huge octopus emerged from the depths, one that was soon vanquished by the brave Golden Knight. Hardcore fans might be waiting for the game to start, but activations like this can be mesmerizing and unforgettable, especially for younger fans.

These are just a few of the many companies, mature and start-up alike, that are changing the fan experience, across sports and around the world. For anyone in the sports marketing or technology business, it's important to understand all these trends and where you and your company might fit in. In our case, it's all about creating immersive, interactive experiences for fans, both on-site and increasingly beyond the field or stadium as well. The best projects for us are the ones where it all comes together. As I've described in this book, it starts with the broadest understanding of a team or brand and how they want to engage with their fans, from before the game to during the game to even after the game. What are the values that drive the team or brand? From there, it's about creating a great experience for the fan, for the team, and for the brand. Once it's envisioned, you need best practices and a great team to bring it all together. One of those projects where it all came together for us and our client was one we recently completed for the Columbus Blue Jackets, an NHL expansion team founded in 2000.

REIMAGINING THE FAN ZONE AT THE COLUMBUS BLUE JACKETS

Starting in 2019, the Columbus Blue Jackets had big plans for their twentieth anniversary in 2020. As part of an upgrading of their stadium, they wanted to completely overhaul their social lounge or fan zone. We were on a short list of vendors that they reached out to talk about a potential renovation plan. Step one for us, of course, is **Discovery**, and that started with doing a site survey. I flew out to Columbus and did a full walk-through of the arena and concourse. Team officials showed me the location they were most interested in renovating, but I had some more basic questions first, such as: What is your brand messaging?

At the time, they did not have much of a message outside of "Hey, this is the twentieth anniversary of our organization, so 2020 is going to be the year that we unveil the new, upgraded stadium." This allowed us to get creative and brainstorm with the Blue Jackets team about the broader message and goals of the fan zone. At the time, their focus was more on younger fans and on creating more kid-friendly activations. The existing space had a carpeted street hockey rink, but it was more like a playpen for kids running around with hockey sticks. They also had a very old photo booth kiosk and this very clunky, oversize hockey slap shot game, made mostly of metal with a plastic bubble over the top. It was just this mechanical contraption, and it felt like it needed oil after each game. The overall aesthetic of the fan zone was like a college frat house for kids, circa 1983.

After our site visit, we flew back to Philadelphia and began to render out some ideas and concepts. We packaged that together into a presentation and sent it to them in February 2020. They loved it and said that they wanted to take it to the next step in terms of formalizing the project into a scope-of-work contract. Weeks later, the Covid pandemic hit, the world changed, and the project, like everything else in sports and life, was put on hold.

In early 2022, they reengaged with us to reimagine the fan zone and try to pick up where we had left off. But a lot had changed in those two years. Many of the Blue Jackets' staff members were new. Not one person whom we communicated with in 2019 was part of the new team. But someone there digging through some old files had found our presentation and reached out to us. But we were essentially starting from square one. They kicked off a new competitive request-for-proposal process, so again we jumped on a plane and headed out to Columbus in April 2022 to give a new dog and pony show. Ryan Chenault, the vice president of marketing, was now leading the project, and there was a lot more intention behind the effort. That led to important questions such as *What is your brand message and what are the core values that you want this space to have? In an ideal scenario, what can we encompass in this designated footprint that's going to achieve your goals?*

Through asking these probing questions, a few things came to light. One insight was that e-sports was a big initiative for their organization. The Columbus Blue Jackets were one of few NHL teams that had their own gaming team, called CBJ Gaming. So a part of their messaging was that they wanted to promote e-sports activity throughout the community. Another key priority was this concept of "Sticks in Hands." This was the slogan behind their community outreach program to support youth hockey in the community to promote hockey in the greater Columbus area. The team's practice facility was attached to Nationwide Arena, but they would open that up for youth or high school teams.

For us, that insight was helpful because it helped guide us in thinking of creative concepts. We began to think about how Topgolf had revolutionized the staid world of driving ranges by combining a physical activity, hitting a golf ball, with a lot of digital and social interaction. We wanted to do something similar for hockey. We thought, *Why not shoot a puck at a virtual, on-screen goalie?*

But unlike a home run game with a stationary wall or a field goal game with a fixed set of goal posts, the goalie would need to react to the speed and position of the shot. Using new technology, we thought this was possible. We would employ 260 frames per second camera sensors that could track the speed and the location of the puck, which in this case would be a street hockey ball. Using AI, the goalie would then react to the shot. But, of course, we didn't want our goalie to be perfect, just good enough to stop most of but not all the shots, just like a real goalie. A digital scoreboard would show how the player was performing. We called it the Slapshot Challenge and offered other shooting games like a speed challenge or target practice. It seemed like the best sticks-in-hand activation outside of being on the ice.

We also developed the concept for a Goalie Challenge, where we would flip the script and the fan would serve as goalie while virtual players hit foam pucks at them. Fans would be fully geared up just like they were on the ice. Once again, using AI, we could gauge the difficulty of the shots by the skills of the goalie and track goals scored.

We wanted to incorporate e-sports in some way, and so we developed a way to piggyback off another stadium project, which was redesigning the players' locker rooms. What fan would not want to tour the locker room before a game? Therefore, we decided to bring the locker room to the fan, building out a smaller but otherwise exact replica in our fan zone and then staging e-sports gaming consoles throughout the locker room.

As a fan entered the space, they would have a one-to-one feel of being in the player locker room, but then could play *NHL 23* from EA Sports. We also planned a series of Morphing Stations where fans could either "pose with the pro" or try on a virtual jersey. Fans could log in to the fan zone with a QR code, which would enable them to retrieve their photos and post them on social media. It would also allow the team to learn who was using the fan zone and for which activations. A social media board would show all the postings in real time.

Our rendering called for two slap shot games, a goalie challenge, the player locker room with e-sports consoles, Morphing Stations, and a large three-foot-by-three-foot video media wall. Through taking a holistic approach and understanding the client's objectives, our discovery and design process helped produce the winning proposal, and we were chosen to move forward with the redesign of the Columbus Blue Jackets Fan Zone.

This was the summer of 2022, and the team wanted the space ready for the 2022–2023 season, just five short months away. First, the existing space needed to be demolished, which took longer than we expected. Next, we needed to specify where we would need data drops, power outlets, or speaker wires. To make sure the deployment was successful, we had to get very specific with our requirements before anything was built. That always presents its own challenge because you can put specifications on paper and take all the measurements, but then when you get on-site, you realize that this stud is four inches off and now that throws off the measurements for a whole new wall that we had started to build. Meanwhile, we are dependent on local subcontractors to get the work done according to our specs and time frame.

Like most of our projects, it was 100 percent bespoke, and it got us out of our comfort zone in terms of project management and the amount of work we had to do to get the project completed on time. It was a complete renovation, and we had to work closely with the carpenter, the general contractor, our fabricator, and others, all of them implementing new technology.

By January 2023, we were on-site for a full week getting everything finalized. Our understanding was that the initial launch would be more of a soft launch, not quite a grand opening, and that we could make any refinements or tweaks throughout the course of the season. The problem was the team and the media started to get wind of the new space, and excitement was building.

> WE WERE DOING OUR BEST AND, AS ALWAYS, BEING TRANS-PARENT WITH THE CLIENT AND SETTING CLEAR EXPECTATIONS.

Throughout that whole week, we were trying to finish everything, but we kept getting bombarded by news media and other preopening events. We were super stressed because certain elements were not 100 percent yet. For example, the sensors on the slap shot game were not tracking accurately. We were doing our best and, as always, being transparent with the client and setting clear expectations. Still, they just kept funneling local news stations through the space.

Finally, the day arrived to do an executive walk-through of the new space before the formal opening to fans. We were not fully ready yet, but everything worked out for the executives, and they were pleased. The space looked phenomenal, and there were some minor tweaks that the user wouldn't even notice. For example, in the Goalie Challenge, we had an AI sensor in the net that would register if the puck went past the goalie and into the net. But that element was not functioning as accurately as we wanted. Still, for the executives trying it out, they were like, "OMG, pucks are shooting out at me! This is a lot of fun," even if the scores were not being tallied completely accurately. This, we felt, could be fixed before opening day.

Next, they did a VIP launch with about 1,500 fans, and it was amazing. Everything was working great. We thought, *This is going to be awesome.* Finally, we felt like we were ready for opening day and the influx of thirty thousand fans. There was only one problem: the Slapshot Challenge stopped working properly.

The slap shot game presented a unique challenge: How do you accurately track the velocity and direction of a street hockey ball that is being hit hard by a hockey stick and traveling at a high rate of speed over a very short distance? As we studied the case of Topgolf, we learned that they use an RFID chip embedded in the ball that can be picked up by sensors on the course. But driving a golf ball and hitting a hockey puck (or in this case, street hockey ball) has a distinct difference: time. It takes several seconds for a golf ball to reach its destination and for Topgolf, the only thing that matters is recording the flight of the ball, where it lands, and where it rolls to. Capturing the velocity and trajectory from the point of impact is not that important. In our case, it was critical. If we had a stationary goalie, we could just record where the hockey ball is striking the screen. But who wants to try and score against a goalie who is standing still and not reacting to the puck? Instead, we needed to instantly record the velocity and direction of the shot so that we could use AI to have the goalie react in real time. This was not easy to do.

Our solution was to use our high-speed cameras to instantly capture the velocity and direction of the hockey balls. The technology was similar to what is used in a motion capture suit, which is used in some VR experiences to capture a user's exact movements. In that case, the motion capture suits are covered with small reflective orbs that reflect light. Those reflections can be captured by the high-speed camera to record rapid movements. Our problem was that we could not affix these reflective orbs to a hockey ball because they would shatter when struck at high speed by a hockey stick.

Our creative workaround was to use reflective stickers instead. We tried the reflective stickers affixed to the hockey ball and, to our great relief, found that it was tracking very accurately. It was like magic to the user that it was working well. Over time, however, we noticed that through repeated whacking by a hockey stick, the surface of the reflective tape was getting worn away and the tracking would degrade. That, too, was an easy fix, we thought. We could order new balls or refurbish old ones and always have a fresh batch on hand. Scuffed or worn hockey balls could quickly be replaced.

The problem we now faced is that our existing stock of balls was already worn down just through all the media events and "preopenings" that we had hosted over the previous few weeks. And our stock of reflective tape had already been used up as well. With our formal opening day set for Saturday night, we ordered ninety new balls and one thousand stickers on Friday for next-day delivery.

As Saturday rolled around, we arrived at the arena early to start on our final integration. By late morning, the balls and stickers had still not arrived, but we thought, *No problem, we have all day. They will get here.* Before too long, however, it was four o'clock, and gates were opening at six o'clock. By that point, the Slapshot Challenge was not working at all because the balls were just completely scuffed and not tracking accurately. Panic was starting to set in. We called FedEx, who said that they had tried to make a delivery attempt in the morning but that the shipment was now back on a truck headed back to the FedEx facility. I went down to the shipping dock and spoke to the security guard, and he said that no FedEx truck had arrived all day.

It was now five o'clock. Gates were opening in less than an hour. My client reminded me of what was at stake. "James," he said, "this has to be a great experience. We have ESPN here. We have social media influencers here. This has to work."

I told my colleague to drive over to the FedEx facility and demand to get the package off the truck. Somehow, we tracked down the driver of the FedEx truck, and after searching the truck, there was still no package to be found. It was now 5:45 p.m. We were fifteen minutes away from the gates opening.

As it turns out, our technical producer was getting all his tools and equipment packed up because we were leaving the next day to work on another activation. As he was staging his equipment at the freight dock, he saw a box labeled "MVP Interactive." He took a picture of the box and sent it to me via a Slack message. "Hmm, what's this?" he texted. "I don't know," I responded, "but get it up here ASAP."

Of course, it turned out to be the shipment of the new balls and reflective tape. With five minutes to spare, we got everything running properly, and the opening was a huge success. Our client, Ryan Chenault, saw me and could not believe we had all pulled it off successfully. High fives and hugs followed.

I stayed in the arena for about an hour, but then I thought, *I just need to get out of here and clear my head.* It happened to be the first round of the NFL playoffs, and the Eagles were playing the New York Giants. I found an Irish pub, ordered a beer, and started watching my Eagles. Ryan texted me and asked, "Are you okay? Things looked a little dicey for you there." I responded with, "No, I'm fine. I'm feeling much better now."

I felt even better when the Eagles went on to trounce the Giants 38–7. High fives and hugs.

THE FUTURE OF IMMERSIVE EXPERIENCES

WE SPOKE BEFORE ABOUT TECHNOLOGY HYPE cycles, and there is no question that we have entered a new one with the introduction of ChatGPT. Released in November 2022 by the start-up OpenAI, ChatGPT grew to 100 million users by January 2023, making it the fastest-growing consumer application ever. The ChatGPT hype cycle was officially on.

ChatGPT is a so-called chat bot: you can ask it questions, and then it answers back. This had been done before, but never in such a way where the "chat" was like you were communicating with a real human being, albeit a highly informed one. But ChatGPT goes far beyond lifelike communications. It can write and debug computer code, write a student essay, or compose music. It can even mimic the style of celebrity CEOs and make a business pitch. Soon, some pundits were claiming that ChatGPT would replace programmers, writers, musicians, or even, God forbid, investment bankers.

We immediately started using ChatGPT in our business, first focused on practical applications like refining our search engine optimization (SEO) strategies or writing blogs or even emails. I have one salesperson who loves to write long emails. I gave him a homework assignment. Log in to ChatGPT and ask it to write a three-sentence paragraph expressing your main points. He tried it, and it worked amazingly well. I don't see ChatGPT replacing any of our salespeople or anyone else any time soon, but I do think it can help make us more efficient in our work, whether writing emails or computer code.

ChatGPT is just one part of a broader AI revolution, one that will have a profound effect on immersive experiences. As just one example, Nvidia has recently introduced its NeRF platform, which can take 2D images and rapidly transform them into 3D immersive worlds. This has immediate implications for us as it allows us to more rapidly transport a participant into a more lifelike experience, whether swinging for the fences or kicking a field goal. Rapid advancements in cameras and, most importantly, processing power will make our immersive experiences easier and faster to deploy and with far less hardware required.

Also, Apple recently released a mixed reality headset, which allows for virtual, augmented, or mixed reality experiences. Like many new technologies, it came with a high price point, $3,000, but we expect this to come down over time and to become more mainstream. This could change the sports viewing experience. Even today, many fans glance down at their iPhone during a game to view live stats or other analytics. The Apple headset, linked to your iPhone, will allow you to see this information without missing any of the action of the field. Also, we are likely to see more on-the-field cameras that can deliver a unique perspective for fans. Like helmet cams in Formula One that allow you to see what the drivers sees streaming along at two hundred miles per hour, you can imagine similar technologies in other sports. Even if helmet cams can never quite survive the crush of a football helmet, you could see other on-the-field or on-the-court cameras giving fans a more direct view of the action.

In our world of creating immersive experiences at sports and other venues, we see AR increasingly being used to create "portals" to enhance the fan's game-day experience. In our Columbus Blue Jackets installation, we re-created the upgraded locker room in our fan zone, but you can imagine a day soon when you can tour the whole stadium using AR. You could imagine, during halftime, using your phone to go on a scavenger hunt virtually around the stadium, competing against other fans.

In terms of other future immersive experiences, we could see second-screen engagements emerging, where on-the-field data and tracking of player performance can be immediately replicated, through AI, into a digital experience. In some ways, you could gamify the action in the game. Imagine you're on a mobile app, for example, and rather than viewing the game with actual athletes, you choose to have Pokémon characters playing instead. You could have all the characters of Pokémon playing in front of you in real time based on what the actual athletes are doing on the field.

Even now, broadcasts are featuring a couple of games a year where they're putting augmented reality images on the television. So when a player scores a touchdown, for example, a slime celebration appears. This might not show up on the main broadcast network, but it might on another channel, like Nickelodeon. You are starting to see the blending of reality with digital imagery.

AI is also pushing the envelope for what's known as deepfake engagements, the ability to interact with fictional or historical figures just like you were talking to them with their characteristics and likeness. You could imagine an immersive experience where you are talking to Vince Lombardi or Tom Landry, or where you are taking a pitch from Sandy Koufax or catching a touchdown pass from Roger Staubach. Or imagine choosing the voice of your own broadcaster. Tony Romo might be providing color commentary of an NFL football team, but to you it sounds like the legendary Jack Whitaker, the great announcer for the Philadelphia Eagles in the 1970s and '80s.

> AI IS CERTAINLY IN A HYPE CYCLE, BUT WE SEE IT AS MORE OF A UTILITY, WHICH WE CAN USE TO POWER MORE ENGAGING AND MORE IMMERSIVE EXPERIENCES.

AI is certainly in a hype cycle, but we see it as more of a utility, which we can use to power more engaging and more immersive experiences. One of its powers is personalization. Advanced analytics and the speed of processing make it possible to know your preferences, your emotions, and your interests and then personalize the experience for you. We see AI being a driving force in creating new, more personalized experiences for our clients and fans, and also in helping to overcome many of the technology and operational challenges we have faced. For example, we work a lot with 3D cameras, and we're beholden to the capabilities of the hardware in terms of what the camera can capture. But if you add a layer of AI to that as either firmware or software, the accuracy and tracking of the camera improves tremendously. AI has the power to strengthen and improve many of the devices we are already using. We see it as a performance-enhancing supplement to our immersive experiences, in a positive way, and not the kind that gets you banned from sports.

These new technologies, whether AI, advanced analytics, or mixed reality, will serve as a supplement in another way: they will always supplement and never replace the action on the field, on the court, on the racetrack, or on the ice. You can gamify or augment athletic competition to make it more entertaining or engaging, but you can never replace the roar of a crowd when Tyreek Hill breaks open down the sidelines and Patrick Mahomes hits him with a perfect pass for a touchdown. The metaverse will never give that experience of sitting at the ballpark on a balmy evening, the moon shining bright, the smell of hot dogs and popcorn, the bark of the beer vendor, and the crack of the bat as forty thousand fans rise to their feet to see if this one makes it over the wall.

If the global pandemic taught us anything, it's that humans crave interaction with other humans. Almost all our immersive experiences have a social element to them, and not just the social media kind, the chance to have your friends watch you hit a home run, the chance to meet new friends in a fan zone, the chance to share your experiences with friends and family. In this way, too, technology is always a supplement, and never a replacement, for fostering those social connections, that spirit of being part of a community of fans. Beyond the jumbotron lies an exciting new world, a world of new technology and immersive experiences, but still a world where the thrill of athletic competition and the importance of social interaction remain paramount.

ACKNOWLEDGMENTS

MOM, YOUR UNWAVERING FAITH IN ME, EVEN WHEN I doubted myself, has been a source of strength throughout my life. Your moral compass and unwavering commitment to doing what's right has been an inspiration to me, and I am proud to have inherited those values from you. You have instilled in me the importance of considering others, which has translated to becoming a servant leader to my team.

My beautiful wife, Heidi, you have changed me in so many ways, and I am forever grateful for your presence in my life. Your undying support, sage advice, and infectious enthusiasm for all that life has to offer have made such an impact. You are one of the few guarantees in life that I can always count on, and for that, I am truly blessed. I love you.

Lola, my dear daughter, you are my greatest source of inspiration. Watching you grow and learn has been one of the greatest joys of my life, and I am so proud of the person you are becoming. I promise to always be present, to build things that make you proud, and to show you that anything is possible. You are my greatest achievement, and I love you more than words could ever express.

To my amazing team members, I am truly grateful for the support and dedication you have shown throughout this journey. Your unyielding belief, even during the most challenging moments, has been instrumental in helping us achieve our goals. You are the backbone of MVP's success. Your hard work, dedication, and commitment to excellence have been the driving force behind the success of our projects. I am honored to lead such a talented group of individuals, and I am proud of the work we have accomplished together.

To my supporters and investors, whether it was one dollar or your time, your investment has enabled me to turn my dreams into a reality and has allowed me to bring these ideas to life. Your confidence in me has been a driving force behind our success, and I will continue to work tirelessly to deliver the results that you expect and deserve. Your faith in me has not gone unnoticed, and I am committed to delivering value and returns on your investment. Thank you for partnering with me on this journey, and I look forward to continuing to work together to achieve our shared goals.

To Rob's Garage: I cannot express enough gratitude for the lifetime of laughter and unforgettable experiences we have shared together. From our teenage years to now, you have been a constant source of support. Our friendship is a testament to the unbreakable bond we have formed over the years, and I am truly grateful for each and every one of you. The fact that we have remained as close as we have for so many years is a testament to the strength of our bond and our willingness to support each other through thick and thin. I am grateful for the memories we have created and look forward to many more in the years to come. My love and gratitude for all of you are eternal.

CONTACT

MVP INTERACTIVE is an extended-reality technology company that creates immersive experiences to amplify your brand by blending real world and digital environments. We specialize in building augmented, virtual, and mixed reality consumer-engagement experiences across sports, retail, entertainment, media, gaming, healthcare, and more. At MVP Interactive, anything is possible. We service brands, sports teams, and marketing agencies and have worked with some of the leading brands across the globe!

For business inquiries please contact us at
https://mvp-interactive.com/about-us/
MVP Interactive
8 Letitia St. #104
Philadelphia, PA 19106

(267) 273-0176 | **info@mvp-interactive.com**
Follow us across all social platforms: **@mvpinteractive**

For speaking engagements, or to contact James directly,
please visit his website: **www.jamesgiglio.com**

james@mvp-interactive.com | jamesgiglio@gmail.com | info@mvp-interactive.com

 @jamesgiglio

 @jamesgiglio

 @jamesgigliohaha

www.linkedin.com/in/%F0%9F%8E%A4-james-giglio-16a8715/

ABOUT THE AUTHOR

JAMES GIGLIO, an expert in creating fan experiences, is the founder and CEO of MVP Interactive, an extended-reality technology company that builds and executes best-in-class immersive experiences to amplify brands across sports, universities, retail, entertainment, and enterprise-level organizations. James's vision in linking technology to fan engagement has been paramount to the growth of the company and has led MVP Interactive to develop products for some of the world's largest brands, sports teams, and leagues. His clients include the NFL, the MLB, the NBA, the MLS, Coca-Cola, Anheuser-Busch, AT&T, Cornell University, the Columbus Blue Jackets, Graceland, and many more. James regularly shares his insight on fan experiences at prestigious events including AWE, National Sports Forum, Experiential Marketing Summit, Digital LA, Digital Hollywood, VR/AR Association Global Summit, NHL league meetings in 2019, Sports Tech Tokyo, AB Bud Light NFL Summit, SportTechie Horizon Summit, and others.

Printed in the USA
CPSIA information can be obtained
at www.ICGtesting.com
JSHW021640051223
53229JS00001BA/102

9 781642 259032